OPAL
A New Musical Adventure

by Robert Lindsey Nassif

Based on the Childhood Diary of
Opal Whiteley (aka Françoise D'Orleans)
written at age seven

Winner of the Richard Rodgers Award

SAMUEL FRENCH, INC.
45 WEST 25TH STREET   NEW YORK 10010
7623 SUNSET BOULEVARD HOLLYWOOD 90046
LONDON   TORONTO

Amateurs wishing to arrange for the production of OPAL must make application to SAMUEL FRENCH, INC., at 45 West 25th Street, New York, NY 10010, giving the following particulars:

    (1) The name of the town and theatre or hall of the proposed production.
    (2) The maximum seating capacity of the theatre or hall.
    (3) Scale of ticket prices.
    (4) The number of performances intended and the dates thereof.
    (5) Indicate whether you will use an orchestration or simply a piano.

Upon receipt of these particulars SAMUEL FRENCH, INC., will quote terms and availability.

Stock royalty quoted on application to SAMUEL FRENCH, INC., 45 West 25th Street, New York, NY 10010.

For all rights than other those stipulated above, apply to William Morris Agency, Inc., 1350 Avenue of the Americas, New York, NY 10019, Attn: Peter Franklin.

An orchestration consisting of:
    Piano/vocal score
    Percussion
will be loaned two months prior to the production ONLY on receipt of the royalty quoted for all performances, the rental fee and a refundable deposit. The deposit will be refunded on the safe return to SAMUEL FRENCH, INC. of all materials loaned for the production.

Printed in the U.S.A.

ISBN 0 573 69392 7

iv

ACKNOWLEDGMENTS

Special thanks to:

Buzz McLaughlin,
Matt Williams and the New Harmony Project
Virginia Dajani,
John Guare,
Stephen Sondheim
The American Academy and Institute of Arts and Letters
    for the Richard Rodgers Award,
W.H. McBryde and the Official Solicitor to the Supreme
    Court of Protection,
Bill Grossman
Beaumont Glass,
Elizabeth Bradburne Lawrence,
John R. Webb,
Tim Jerome, John Znidarsic and the National Music
    Theater Network
Carolyn Rossi Copeland, Scott Harris, Janet Watson,
    Joshua Rosenblum, Peter Harrison, Michael Bottari,
    Ron Case, and all involved in the Lamb's production.

Opal premiered in New York City on March 12, 1992, at the Lamb's Theatre, Carolyn Rossi Copeland, Producing Director, with the following cast:

SADIE McKIBBEN ....Marni Nixon
OPAL (at alternating performances) ...Eliza Clark & Tracy Spindler
THE MAN THAT WEARS GRAY NECKTIES ...Mark Goetzinger
THE MAMMA ....Louisa Flaningam
THE GIRL THAT HAS NO SEEING ....Mimi Bessette
THE THOUGHT-GIRL WITH THE FAR-AWAY LOOK IN HER
   EYES ....Pipa Winslow
NARRATORS ....Reed Armstrong, Sarah Knapp,
                                              Alfred Lakeman, Judy Malloy

(*Understudies*: Kathleen Bloom, Ray Leutters, Maureen McNamera,
   Regina O'Malley, Carol Skarimbas, Jean Tafler)

Directed by: Scott Harris
Musical Director: Joshua Rosenblum
Musical Staging: Janet Watson
Scenic Design: Peter Harrison
Costume Design: Michael Bottari/Ron Case
Lighting Design: Don Ehman
Sound Design: Jim Van Bergen
Assistant Scenic Design: Steven E. Johnson
General Manager: Nancy Nagel Gibbs
Production Manager: Clark Cameron
Production Stage Manager: Sandra M. Franck

Piano/Conductor: Joshua Rosenblum
Piano/Associate Conductor: Lynn Crigler
Drums/Percussion: Kerry Meads
(*Subs*: David Caldwell, Eric Phinney)

CHARACTERS

THE PRINCIPALS

The principals remain in character throughout the piece, while the narrators assume various roles.

OPAL (FRANÇOISE). A-seven-year old aristocratic girl; petite, enchanting, yet with spunk; should speak in a cultured manner perhaps with a very slight English accent, but not a French accent; should be cast as young and small as possible; must have a sweet, legitimate singing voice, not a belt voice. (Bb to F#)

THE MAMMA (MRS. POTTER). An embittered, work-worn woman; mid-forties; might be cast with a comedienne who can also play pathos; there is comedy in the role, but the mamma must be a real person, not a caricature; legitimate mezzo-soprano voice—not a chest or belt voice. (Middle C to D, possibly high G in choral numbers)

THE MAN THAT WEARS GRAY NECKTIES (ANDREW GIVENS). A lumberjack; shy, self-effacing, manly yet mild mannered, and very likable; mid-thirties to early forties, a strong, natural-sounding baritone voice; may be cast with a country singer. (Bb to F) This actor should also play ANGEL FATHER—Opal's real father; a French aristocrat; wears an elegant turn of the century morning coat and top hat.

SADIE McKIBBEN. An "elderly" Scottish scrub-woman; an eccentric outcast, a mystic, an earth-mother; sage-like, but with a childlike sense of joy; must have a fine, legitimate soprano voice. (Bb to high Ab)

THE GIRL THAT HAS NO SEEING (SELENA). A blind woman; in her twenties, painfully repressed, waif-like and fragile; drably dressed; must have a beautiful, natural-sounding mezzo-soprano voice—with an element of musical theatre chest/belt voice in it. (Bb to Eb)

THE THOUGHT-GIRL WITH THE FAR-AWAY LOOK IN HER EYES. The daughter of the lumbermill owner; poetically beautiful, modest, and endearing; socially awkward and easily embarrassed; she works in the cookhouse; though her father is relatively wealthy, she should be seen doing chores, like the others; must have an extremely beautiful, legitimate soprano voice. (B to high A) This actress should also play ANGEL MOTHER—Opal's real mother; she wears an elegant turn-of-the-century gown and a hat with a veil; perhaps carries a parasol.

THE NARRATORS

Minimum: 2 men, 2 women (evenly mixed voices—soprano, mezzo-soprano/alto, tenor, baritone/bass)

The narrators tell the story to the audience and assume various roles. They are guiding spirits, who sometimes observe the action of the play, invisible to the principal players. At other times, they don bits of costumes and become various lumber camp characters. They also change scenery, provide sound-effects, and create theatrical magic.

They must have very fine voices; be rugged and sincere, individualistic types; be able to play comedy as well as drama; twenties to early forties, strong, athletic.

The men must be especially burly and masculine to convey the ruggedness of lumber camp life and to counterbalance the large number of female leading characters. If more than four narrators are used, give preference to additional men for the same reasons, then add women if desired.

One of the men must be able to make realistic pig noises—grunts, snorts, whimpers, etc.

The narrators' basic costume is lumber camp garb. They don hats, scarves, glasses, etc. to portray specific characters.

The narrators portray:

MAN. A rough dock worker.

PETER PAUL RUBENS. A pig; a male narrator should be his "voice," providing the appropriate grunts and squeals. The pig is never actually seen. Opal mimes petting him. Occasionally we "see" him in the chaos he generates.

LUMBER CAMP FOLKS/MILL TOWN PEOPLE. Used interchangeably to refer to the lumberjacks and pioneering women who inhabit the lumber camp with its shanties, bunk houses, ranch house gathering place, cook house dining hall and sawmill.

THE GOSSIP SISTERS. Two comical spinsters who speak simultaneously most of the time. Two female narrators don half-glasses to transform themselves into these characters. In the Lamb's production, the designers also had them don Victorian capes.

SELENA'S MOTHER. Heard, but not seen. A female narrator provides her voice, while turned upstage standing apart from the action.

SCHOOL TEACHER. Seen from Opal's perspective—she is gigantic and comically frightening.

FELIX MENDELSSOHN. A mouse. He is never seen. We see Opal mime petting him, and she or a female narrator provides the squeaks.

GENERAL STORE OWNER. An old, lecherous grandpappy. Wears a visor and a shop apron.

SQUARE DANCE CALLER

THE YOUNG HUSBAND OF ELSIE

BARBER

TIME & PLACE

1904, A lumber camp in Oregon.

The play is presented by a group of narrators, who tell the story through mime, imagination, sound effects, and by transforming themselves into various characters.

The production should be simple, spare, and magically theatrical. The things of "reality and work" are seen (saws, brooms, axes, crates, barrels, buckets, a washtub, etc.). The animals are unseen. The actors use mime in relating to them.

SCENE LOCATIONS AND SONGS

Sequence Five: Winter
The Lumber Camp
"To Conquer the Land" reprise ....Full Company
"Angel Mother, Angel Father" reprise......................Opal

Sequence Six: Spring
The Homes of the Thought-Girl and the Girl That Has No Seeing
"Someone".. The Thought-Girl and
The Girl That Has No Seeing

Sequence Seven: Summer
Mrs. Potter's Lumber Shanty
"The Locket" .... The Mamma

The Forest Cathedral

Sadie McKibben's Shanty

The General Store

The Forest Path, The Barber Shop and the House of the Thought-Girl
"Everybody's Looking for Love".......Neckties and Company

The Deep Forest
"Why Do I See God?"... Sadie

Sequence Eight: Days Later
The Lumber Camp

The Charred Remains of the Forest Cathedral

xii

PROLOGUE — Early 1904

SETTING: A lumber camp and pine tree forest. An all-purpose playing area laid with rough-hewn planks, edged with tall, rough poles to represent the forest. No full room settings or complex scene changes. A simple chair or a few props are used to indicate place.

The Far-Away Lands

[Music Cue #1: MAKE EARTH GLAD]

We see a distant dream vision of a little GIRL being presented with a music box by her attentive PARENTS. The GIRL winds the music box then opens it. It begins repeating a simple theme. Perhaps this takes place behind a scrim.
The NARRATORS, in lumber camp garb, assemble—one or two carry lanterns.

FRANÇOISE and PARENTS. (*Singing to the music box*)
FIND THE WAY TO MAKE EARTH GLAD
AND EARTH APPROACHES HEAVEN
NARRATORS. (*Throughout the play, separate lines are assigned to different narrators; speaking to the audience.*)
Our story is about a real person.
It is taken from an actual diary written many years ago by a seven year old girl—
an aristocratic, silver spoon child named Françoise—
written as she spent her first year in a strange new world.

13

She said she never knew for certain who her parents
were or where they were from.

She only remembered a princess she called mother,

and a noble man she called father,

and that they lived for a few happy years in the
faraway lands.

ALL.
FIND THE WAY TO MAKE EARTH GLAD,
AND EARTH APPROACHES
AND EARTH APPROACHES
AND EARTH APPROACHES
AND EARTH APPROACHES —

NARRATORS.
until she arrived in Oregon
in the summer of 1904.

*(A sudden BLACKOUT. [Music Cue #1A] A deafening
crash of THUNDER. Blinding LIGHTNING. A
ship's SIREN blares.)*

A Shipwreck

*(The NARRATORS mime a shipwreck on a stormed-
tossed ocean. A search LIGHT blinds us from
upstage, so we cannot see clearly. It sweeps from side
to side, creating a bizarre shadow play on the scrim.*
*In silhouette, we see the little GIRL being torn from the
arms of her parents. SHOUTS for help. STRUGGLE.
FRENZY. Fighting for life.)*

FRANÇOISE. Maman! Papa! Where are you?!

(A MAN grabs her and picks her up roughly.)

MAN. The ship's goin' under!
FRANÇOISE. Maman! Papa!

MAN. Git in the lifeboat!

FRANÇOISE. No! I want my mother and father!

MAN. It's too late! They's gone!

FRANÇOISE. Gone where?!

MAN. (*Leaving with her.*) Just gone! Now, git in the lifeboat while there's still time!

FRANÇOISE. No!

MAN. Git in, or you'll drown, too!!

FRANÇOISE. (*Her voice joins the terrible din of wailing.*) Maman!!! Papa!!! Where are you?!!!

(*More TURMOIL and CONFUSION. PASSENGERS cling and cry. Fade to:*)

SEQUENCE ONE — Summer of 1904

(*Night. A THUNDERSTORM. LIGHTNING. THUNDER. A WOLF howls in the distance.*)

Mrs. Potter's Lumber Shanty

(*This scene is DARK and claustrophobic. We cannot as yet discern the locale—not until the next scene.
[Music Cue # 1B]
More THUNDER and LIGHTNING. The sound of RAIN on the roof of a shack. In the dark, we hear POUNDING on the door. One or more of the NARRATORS observes the scene from the surrounding darkness.*)

MAN. (*Gruffly.*) Mrs. Potter! Open up! Mrs. Potter!

MRS. POTTER. (*Lighting a lantern.*) Who's out there at this hour?!

(*SHE opens the door cautiously—this and other similar stage directions should be done in mime with no literal*)

*doorways, etc.. Here, for instance, the "door" in the
Lamb's production was an opening between two
sections of ragged scrim cloth hanging mid-stage.
A rough looking MAN barges in.)*

MRS. POTTER. Who are you?!
MAN. (*Menacingly.*) I work the shipping dock in
Portland with a fella that knows ya. ... He told me ya just
moved here ta this new lumber camp *alone.* Said ya
needed help bad. And here it is.

*(HE whistles. The little GIRL from the prologue looks in
cautiously.)*

MAN. (*Dragging her in through the door.*) Come on,
git in here!

*(The GIRL falls to the floor. We see her for the first time.
SHE is a beautiful child—seven years old—wearing an
elegant lace dress, which is now wet, torn and dirty.)*

MRS. POTTER. (*Suspiciously.*) Who is she?
MAN. (*Takes a swig from a flask.*) There was a
shipwreck. A *foreign* ship. Her folks drowned. I seen
'em. So, seein' how yer husband's run off and ya got
this farm ta run by yerself, I figgered ya needed some
help.
MRS. POTTER. Yup. I need help.
MAN. An' I need twenty-five bucks.
MRS. POTTER. (*A NARRATOR hands her a
shotgun, which she trains on the man.*) Git outa here, the
both a ya!
MAN. (*Grabs the girl and holds her in front of
himself for cover.*) You'll never last the winter without
help!
MRS. POTTER. Maybe not, but I sure as hell don't
buy children. Now, git out!
MAN. (*Starting to leave.*) Yer one tough Missus ...

MRS. POTTER. I have ta be.
MAN. (*Stops; thinks.*) Truth is ... I got nowhere else ta take 'er.
MRS. POTTER. (*Thinks.*) Then ... leave 'er.
NARRATOR. And ...

(*The MAN sets down the girl. HE spits on the floor.*)

NARRATORS. (*In unison.*) ... he did.

(*The MAN exits. MRS. POTTER hands the rifle to a NARRATOR. The NARRATORS exit, leaving MRS. POTTER alone with the frightened CHILD.*)

MRS. POTTER. (*Sizing her up.*) A *foreign* ship, huh? What's the matter? No speaky English? Let's see if ya got some muscle.

(*Though afraid, the CHILD has spirit. SHE pulls away indignantly.*)

MRS. POTTER. I got a feelin' you understand me. Come on. Let's git cha outa them wet clothes.

(*SHE helps the girl remove her dress. As it is pulled off over her head, the CHILD raises her arms regally—she is accustomed to being dressed by servants.*)

MRS. POTTER. Mighty fancy dress. I bet chu never worked a day in yer life. (*Wringing out the wet dress.*) Too bad fer you yer folks never had swimmin' lessons. Now they're gone, gone, gone.
FRANÇOISE. (*Defiantly.*) They are not!
MRS. POTTER. Aha! You do speak English! I thought so!
FRANÇOISE. (*As if shouting a command to a servant.*) Madame, vous n'avez pa le droit de me retenir!

MRS. POTTER. I don't know what you just said, but I didn't like it! From now on, you talk in English, like a normal human bein'!

FRANÇOISE. I don't like you. I don't like it here. And I'm going to find Mother and Father!

MRS. POTTER. Well, there's the door. Help yerself.

FRANÇOISE. I shall! (*FRANÇOISE grabs her dress and marches out into the night.*)

MRS. POTTER. (*Calling after.*) If the timber wolves don't eat cha, the bears will.

(*A crash of THUNDER. WOLF howls. FRANÇOISE runs back in—then quickly tries to hide her fear.*)

MRS. POTTER. Well, either ya decided ta come back, or you got a bad sense a direction. Just remember, yer here ta work. It's what they call a business investment. Yer the investment. An' I mean business.

(*During the following, MRS. POTTER towels off the girl with a blanket.*)

FRANÇOISE. Where is maman et mon père?
MRS. POTTER. What?
FRANÇOISE. Where are Mother and Father?!
MRS. POTTER. (*Callously.*) They're gone, girl.
FRANÇOISE. Gone where?
MRS. POTTER. Up there.
FRANÇOISE. With the angels?
MRS. POTTER. Guess so.
FRANÇOISE. When will they be back?
MRS. POTTER. They won't. They're gone fer good.
FRANÇOISE. I don't believe you!
MRS. POTTER. Fine, don't. But while yer waitin' fer 'em ta come back yer gonna need a place ta stay. That's why ya was brung here ta me. I need help ... You

need a home. (*Pointing to a spot on the floor.*) Ya can sleep right here.

(*The GIRL looks disdainfully at Mrs. Potter, then, wrapped in the blanket, goes to the opposite side of the room and plops down on the floor.*)

MRS. POTTER. Well, if that's the way ya want it ... (*Starting to exit.*) Goodnight—uh, what did ya say yer name was?

[*Music Cue #1C*]
(*The GIRL refuses to respond.*)

MRS. POTTER. No name? (*Still no response.*) Hmph. Then, I reckon I'll have ta give ya one. (*Thinks.*) Let's see.
FRANÇOISE. My name is Françoise.
MRS. POTTER. Fran—what?
FRANÇOISE. Françoise.
MRS. POTTER. I can't remember no foreign sissy name. Now, let's see ... (*A thought.*) I know. I know! I'll call you Opal—after another little girl I used ta know.
FRANÇOISE. Why?
MRS. POTTER. It's a name I ain't said in a while. It might be nice ta hear it again.
FRANÇOISE. ("OPAL") What do I call you?
MRS. POTTER. Me? Well ... why don't cha call me ... mamma.
FRANÇOISE. Why?
MRS. POTTER. It's another a them names I'd like ta hear again.
FRANÇOISE. But it's the name I call my mother.
MRS. POTTER. Well, I'll just borrow it a while 'til she comes back. Goodnight ... Opal. (*SHE exits with the lantern, leaving the girl alone in darkness.*)
OPAL. (*Calling after.*) But, my name is *Françoise.*

[Music Cue #1D]
*(RAIN and WIND. The GIRL creeps across the room to
    see where the mamma went. The NARRATORS enter
    in the dark to observe the action.*
*Suddenly, a blinding flash of LIGHTING and a crash of
    THUNDER. The GIRL lurches backwards and falls to
    the floor, bumping into something in the dark.)*

NARRATORS. *(Tossing a bundle of brown paper at
the girl's feet.)*
   A bundle of old butchers' paper fell to the floor,
(Tossing down crayons.)
   along with three colored wax pencils.
   Suddenly—an idea.
   Huddled on the floor,
   she began to write.

*(As the crayon touches the paper, poignant MUSIC
    begins.)*

[Music Cue #2: ANGEL MOTHER, ANGEL FATHER]

   OPAL. (FRANÇOISE.) *(Writing, but speaking at a
normal rate of speed.)* Dear Angel Mother and Father ...
Maybe you can read my words from where you are.
ANGEL MOTHER,
FLOATING IN THE SKY,
ANGEL FATHER,
HOW I WONDER WHY:

WHY YOU'RE UP IN HEAVEN
DOING ANGEL THINGS.
MOTHER,
FATHER,
HOW CAN I GROW WINGS?

*(Lost in memory, SHE stops writing and comes
    downstage.)*

RIDING YOUR SHOULDERS;
GOING EXPLORES;
LEARNING OF CHOPIN
AND LOUIS QUATORZE.

WALTZING WITH FATHER;
SINGING OUR SONG;
WHY DID YOU LEAVE ME?
DID I DO SOMETHING WRONG?

(As if looking through a window up at the sky:)

ANGEL MOTHER,
WATCHING ME BELOW,
ANGEL FATHER,
HOW I WANT TO KNOW:

HOW CAN I BE NEAR YOU,
NOW YOU'RE WHERE YOU ARE?
MOTHER,
FATHER,
HEAVEN IS SO FAR.

(Her MOTHER and FATHER appear behind her in a distant dream-vision, bathed in celestial light.)

OPAL. (*Speaking out front.*) Maman! Papa! Now that you're in heaven, how can I be with you again? Is there a way?

ANGEL FATHER. (*French accent.*) Françoise, do you remember the music box we gave you on your birthday?

(We hear the MUSIC BOX playing its simple theme.)

OPAL. Yes. But, it was lost in the sea with you.

ANGEL MOTHER. (*An accent of indefinite origin.*)
What was the song the music box played?

OPAL. "Make Earth Glad." (*Singing along with the music box.*)
FIND THE WAY TO MAKE EARTH GLAD,
AND EARTH APPROACHES HEAVEN.

ANGEL FATHER. And that is what you must do to be near us again.

ANGEL MOTHER. Though the music box was lost at sea, its glad-song must not stop playing in your heart.

ANGEL FATHER. We shall be with you again and always—but only if you find the secret way to make earth glad.

OPAL. But, what does that mean? How do I make earth glad?!

ANGEL MOTHER and FATHER. That only you can discover. Search, Françoise. Search for the way.

OPAL, ANGEL MOTHER & FATHER.	NARRATORS.
ANGEL MOTHER, THOUGH THE EARTH IS SAD, ANGEL FATHER, I SHALL MAKE IT GLAD,	(*Hum softly.*)
WHILE YOU AND GALILEO POLISH EVERY STAR.	
MOTHER,	HERE I AM
FATHER,	ALL ALONE.
MOTHER,	HERE I AM
FATHER, ALL. LIFE IS SO LONG,	ON MY OWN.

AND HEAVEN IS
SO FAR ...

*(ANGEL MOTHER and FATHER disappear. The song
ends. [Music Cue #2A]*
*Suddenly, there is a CRASH outside. GRUNTING.
SNORTING.*
*A pig races about the stage. He is not visibly portrayed,
but we "see" him as the NARRATORS chase him,
trying to catch him.)*

NARRATORS. (*Ad-lib chaos.*) Git 'im! Come back
here, you! Look out! (*Etc.*)

*(The pig creates havoc, knocking over everything in its
path—crates, barrels, and people.*
*Finally, the pig calms down and starts rolling in a puddle
of mud. Here, as throughout the play, a male
NARRATOR provides the pig noises while watching
from the sidelines. SNORTING. GRUNTING.
SNUFFLING. A pool of LIGHT defines where the
pig has settled.)*

NARRATORS. (*To audience.*)
Outside the shanty,
a pig broke out of the pigpen
and began rolling in the mud.
Hearing him, Opal climbed quietly out the window.

OUTSIDE THE SHANTY

*(OPAL mimes sneaking outside. SHE approaches the pig
cautiously. HE snorts. SHE jumps back, frightened.)*

OPAL. (*To the pig; mildly scolding; hiding her fear.*)
It's not proper to roll in the mud, you know. (*SHE
approaches him again. SHE kneels by the pig and mimes
petting him timidly. To the pig.*) Are you lost and alone?

Poor thing. (*SQUEAL*.) Don't be afraid. You're not alone anymore. I'm here now. Do you have a name? (*GRUNT*.) No name? (*SNORT*.) Then, I reckon I shall have to give you one.

NARRATORS. And she named him,
using one of the names she had been taught.

OPAL. We're going to be friends forever, (*Thinks ... decides.*) Peter Paul Rubens.

(*A SQUEAL. SHE hugs him. BLACKOUT.*)

SEQUENCE TWO — The Following Weeks

The Lumber camp and Mrs. Potter's Shanty

[Music Cue #3: TO CONQUER THE LAND]

(*MUSICALLY underscored montage of lumber camp life and Opal's first weeks with Mrs. Potter.*
DAWN. The lumber camp awakes. The LUMBER CAMP FOLKS fill the stage. We see them in silhouette. Burly men. Rugged women.)

LUMBER CAMP FOLKS, THE MAMMA, SADIE, GIRL THAT HAS NO SEEING, THE THOUGHT-GIRL, & NECKTIES. (*With strength, dignity, and defiant anger.*)
AND WE RISE,
AND WE WORK,
IN THE BITTER COLD AND DAMP.

AND WE CHOP,
AND WE CLEAR,
AND WE HAUL FROM CAMP TO CAMP.

(*Work begins.*)

AND WE CAME TO TAME THE LAST FRONTIER,
LEAVING ALL THAT'S NEAR AND DEAR,
CAME THIS WAY TO PIONEER,
AND CONQUER THE LAND.

(The LUMBERJACKS construct the camp; sharpen their
   axes; chop trees; and saw with a two-man cross-cut
   saw; etc. The WOMEN scrub; churn; grind; wash;
   cook; etc. Their work movements are in time with the
   music.)

LUMBERJACKS.   **WOMEN.**
AND WE HACK,

                             AND WE SCRUB,
AND WE HEW,

                             AND WE SCRAPE,
AND WE
   ALL.
TETHER, TIE, AND SAW.
LUMBERJACKS.   **WOMEN.**
AND WE GRIND,

                             AND WE STRAIN,
AND WE CLAMP,

                             AND WE POUND,
AND WE WORK
   ALL.
OUR FINGERS RAW.

AND WE CAME TO TAME THE LAST FRONTIER,
CAME TO LIVE WITH STRANGERS HERE,
CAME TO CLEAR AND PIONEER,
AND CONQUER THE LAND.

MAYBE THERE'S A FLOOD.
MAYBE THERE'S A FIRE.
MAYBE THERE'S A LOG-JAM IN THE FLUME.

MAYBE THERE'S A PLAGUE.
MAYBE THERE'S A DROUGHT.
MAYBE ONE MORE LOGGER MEETS HIS DOOM.

LUMBERJACKS.	WOMEN.
AND WE RISE,	
	AND WE RISE,
AND WE WORK,	
	AND WORK.
IN THE BITTER COLD AND DAMP.	
AND WE CHOP,	
	AND WE CHOP,
AND WE CLEAR,	
AND WE HAUL FROM CAMP TO CAMP,	
	AND THERE.

ALL.
(AND THERE) AIN'T A SINGLE THING THAT'S
  SURE,
'CEPT THE SUN AND COW MANURE.
THAT'S THE LIFE YOU LIVE, IF YOU'RE
TO CONQUER THE LAND.

THAT'S THE LIFE YOU LIVE, IF YOU'RE
TO CONQUER THE LAND!

(*The lumber camp FOLKS freeze. LIGHTS focus on
    OPAL.*)

OPAL. (*Out front—to the sky.*) Dear Angel Mother
and Father ... until I find the way to be with you again, I
am staying with someone called "the mamma." The more
I know *her,* the more I miss *you.*

(*First Vignette. OPAL and the MAMMA at breakfast.
    OPAL is now dressed in a drab dress that was sewn*

from an old flour sack. The MAMMA shoves a bowl into Opal's hands, then slops a ladle of oat mush into the bowl.)

THE MAMMA. (MRS. POTTER.) Eat yer grub. It's all you'll git 'til supper.
OPAL. But Madame le Cuisinier always made me crepe l'orange avec patisserie.
THE MAMMA. Uh huh ... Well, this here's *mush*. *(The MAMMA bangs another clump of mush in Opal's bowl.)*

(The LUMBER CAMP FOLKS whistle as THEY go about their work, crossing in front of OPAL, regrouping, etc., suggesting the passage of time.)

OPAL. *(Out front.)* The mamma does not have a cook or a governess or a servant—except for me. She needs lots of helps and has lots of *do's* for me to do.

(Second Vignette. OPAL and the MAMMA by the pig trough.)

THE MAMMA. *(Mimes filling a trough with a heavy bag of feed.)* Now, pay attention. This here is how yer ta slop the hogs. *(Calling.)* Suuuuueeeee! Suuuuueeeeee!
OPAL. Look at Peter Paul Rubens rolling in the mud. I really must teach him some manners, so he can become a gentleman pig .
THE MAMMA. You stupid girl. A pig ain't a pet.
OPAL. Why?
THE MAMMA. Because he is bacon on four legs.
OPAL. What does that mean?
THE MAMMA. It means that once he gits ta be big enough ta make me some money, he's gonna git sold.
OPAL. You can't. Once you get to know him, you'll have so much fondness for him, you'll never sell him.

THE MAMMA. Just exactly where did you come from?

OPAL. I don't know. When I was there, everybody knew where they was, so nobody asked me.

THE MAMMA. Well, I got news fer ya. Yer here now. Yer with me. An' here we work and we sell or we starve. The sooner you git that, the better.

OPAL. I'm only here until I find out how to get to Angel Mother and Father.

THE MAMMA. I told you they ain't comin' back. You can believe me or not. But you better believe this: You are ta stay away from that pig. An' the next time I have ta say that, it'll be with my hand.

OPAL. (*Indignantly.*) He isn't a pig. His *name* is Peter Paul Rubens!

THE MAMMA. Well, come harvest-time, his name is *breakfast*! (*Calling.*) Suuuuueeeeee!

(*The LUMBER CAMP FOLKS whistle and cross the stage as before. Time passes.*)

OPAL. (*Out front.*) The mamma is teaching me to do "chores." I have wants to do things right, for she gets sparky when I do things wrong. Every day, she says to sweep the floor, wash the plates, empty the ashes, scrub the clothes, sew the carpet strings, churn the butter—

(*Third Vignette. OPAL and the MAMMA doing chores.*)

THE MAMMA. —and fetch that pail.

(*OPAL fetches a rug beater.*)

THE MAMMA. No, you stupid girl, not a rug beater. The pail. (*Getting it herself.*) This here is what cha call a *pail*.

OPAL. (*In recognition.*) A bucket.

THE MAMMA. Bucket, pail, same thing! (*Handing OPAL the bucket.*) Here. Now, scrub ... (*OPAL does nothing.*) Ain't chu never scrubbed before?

OPAL. No.

THE MAMMA. (*Huffs. Showing her each item.*) Bucket.

OPAL. (*Unintentionally imitating the mamma's coarse accent.*) Bucket.

THE MAMMA. Brush.

OPAL. Brush.

THE MAMMA. Bon Ami. (*Pronounced crassly as "bahn am´-mee."*)

OPAL. (*Seeing the can; with delight.*) Ah, oui! Je le connais! "Bon ami!" (*Elegant French pronunciation.*)

THE MAMMA. (*Exploding.*) I told you, no more queer talk! (*Shaking the can.*) It's Bon *Ami*!! (*The powder gets in her face. A cough.*)

OPAL. (*Imitating the mamma's vulgar pronunciation.*) "Baaaaahn Am-meee!!" (*A cough.*)

THE MAMMA. (*A slow burn.*) Scrub.

(*OPAL scrubs the floor. We hear the MUSIC box theme.*)

OPAL. (*Out front.*)
FIND THE WAY TO MAKE EARTH GLAD,
AND EARTH APPROACHES HEAVEN.
(*Gets up; comes forward.*)
Every day I do think of those words and wonder what they mean. If I can find the way to make earth glad, you said I would be with you again.

(*Bright MUSIC. The MAMMA hands OPAL a basket of eggs.*)

THE MAMMA. Eggs

OPAL. (*To audience.*) The mamma also has me collect eggs in the henhouse and take them 'round to the folks that buys them.

NARRATORS. (*All; in unison.*) Many folks there be.

A MILL TOWN WOMAN. (*Mimes taking eggs from OPAL; patting her on the head.*) Some is friendly.

A LUMBERJACK. (*Gruffly; to OPAL.*) Some is not!

OPAL. (*Backs away. To audience.*) Like the Gossip Sisters.

(Two FEMALE NARRATORS become the GOSSIP SISTERS.)

GOSSIP SISTERS. (*Two old maids who speak simultaneously. For variety, some of their lines may also be divided between them—one of them starting a sentence and the other finishing it.*) She's a strange little girl. Probably demented. Half of what she says you don't understand, and the other half comes out like she's talking backwards.

OPAL. (*To the GOSSIP SISTERS.*) The ruffles on your dresses are like an oil painting by Rembrandt.

GOSSIP SISTERS. (*Horrified gasp. To audience.*) You see? Demented.

OPAL. (*Out front.*) And some folks is not happy. They have needs. Like the man that wears gray neckties...

(A LUMBERJACK steps forward.)

GOSSIP SISTERS. (*To each other; confidentially.*) ... who needs a *wife*.

OPAL. And the thought-girl with the far-away look in her eyes ...

(A lovely young WOMAN steps forward. SHE is soft and feminine. NECKTIES watches her longingly.)

GOSSIP SISTERS ... who needs a husband and a baby—preferably in that order.

A MALE NARRATOR. *(To audience.)* They met in the general store the first week of logging season. *(HE dons a visor and becomes the crusty old general store owner. Handing a large catalogue to the THOUGHT-GIRL.)* Here ya go, ma'am.

(NECKTIES mimes entering the general store. A little BELL ding-a-lings as HE opens the door.)

NECKTIES. Them new catalogues come in yet?

GENERAL STORE OWNER. Sorry, Mr. Givens. I just gave out the last of 'em.

NECKTIES. Oh.

THOUGHT GIRL. Here. Take mine.

NECKTIES. Oh, no, ma'am, I, uh—*(HE looks at her, suddenly overwhelmed.)*

THOUGHT-GIRL. Please. My father probably has one.

NECKTIES. That's right kind a you. Thank you, Mrs.—uh—

THOUGHT-GIRL. Miss. Miss Ryden.

NECKTIES. Say, Miss Ryden, I seen you servin' once or twice in the cookhouse. Is yer pa one of us shanty boys?

THOUGHT-GIRL. Well, sort of.

GENERAL STORE OWNER. *(Yanking NECKTIES aside.)* Andrew, you moose! Her pa *owns* the whole damn lumbermill.

NECKTIES. Oh, boy. Forgive me, ma'am. I wouldn't a been so familiar if I'd a known you was who ya was—

THOUGHT-GIRL. But I'm not—

NECKTIES. I mean, ya are who ya are—

THOUGHT-GIRL. I mean, you weren't—
NECKTIES. An' if I see another catalogue in the outhouse, it's yers. (*Realizes what he has said. To himself.*) Duuuummmmb.
NARRATORS.
And, shortly after that day,
Miss Ryden began finding bunches of wildflowers—
left on the path outside her home.
NARRATOR. And there is also the girl that has no seeing ...

(*LIGHTS up on SELENA. OPAL is leading her.*)

OPAL. (*Out front.*) ... who needs eyes.
GIRL THAT HAS NO SEEING. I used to see, when I was your age. Then, I lost my sight.
OPAL. Your eyes aren't lost, I can see them. They're just broken.
GIRL THAT HAS NO SEEING. Yes, they are.
OPAL. Maybe I can find a way to fix them.
VOICE OF SELENA'S MOTHER. (*Heard but never seen.*) You keep away from my daughter, you strange little girl!
NARRATOR. (*To audience.*) And then there is Sadie McKibben, an old scrub woman ...

(*LIGHTS up on SADIE McKIBBEN, who is scrubbing clothes with a wash-board and tub. OPAL goes to her.*)

GOSSIP SISTERS. ... who does other peoples wash, if you can imagine. Folks say she's odd—reads tea leaves and foreheads—or something. But she's no seer, she's just senile.
OPAL. Don't you have children, ma'am?
SADIE. No.
OPAL. Why not?

SADIE. I wanted them very much. But, it was not in the stars. And now, I am too old.

OPAL. I know. Why don't I come live with you, until I am with my mother and father again. I can be of helps. And you wouldn't spank me, like the mamma I live with for now.

SADIE. Is she harsh with ye?

OPAL. Yes.

SADIE. Perhaps it's because she needs yir help so much. (*Pause.*) What's your name, child?

OPAL. I don't have one anymore ... I *used* to be Françoise. But now, the mamma calls me *Opal*.

SADIE. (*Touches Opal's face.*) Opal. 'Tis a gem, ye know. Something very rare and very precious.

OPAL. Let me live with you.

SADIE. Perhaps I shall—if it be in the stars. For if there's one thing we all could use, it's a bit of help.

(*That word has struck a chord. OPAL contemplates it as SHE comes to the audience. Lush MUSIC underscores.*)

OPAL. (*Thinking hard.*) ... Help ... (*Suddenly; a revelation.*) Dear Angel Mother and Father ... Now I know what the music box song means. It means I must *help* folks get things they *need*. And then you will come back to me, as soon as I *make earth glad*!

(*The NARRATORS suddenly turn back into the LUMBER CAMP FOLKS.*)

ALL. (*But Opal.*)
MAYBE YOU GET SICK!
MAYBE YOU GET LICE!
MAYBE YOU CHOP OFF ANOTHER TOE!
MAYBE YOU GO BROKE!
MAYBE YOU GO BUST!
MAYBE IS THE ONLY LIFE WE KNOW!

*(As everyone works, the MAMMA tries to teach OPAL to
do more chores. But OPAL has other things on her
mind, and soon disappears in the crowd.)*

ALL.
AND WE CAME—TO—TAME—THE—LAND!

LUMBERJACKS.	**WOMEN.**
AND WE HEAVE,	
	AND WE CUT,
AND WE ROPE,	
	AND WE STITCH,

    ALL.
AND WE SHOVEL, PLOW, AND PLANT.

LUMBERJACKS.	**WOMEN.**
AND WE FORGE,	
	AND WE CARVE,
AND WE BOLT,	
	AND WE NAIL,
AND WE WORK	

    ALL.
FROM "CAN" TO "CAN'T."

(The LUMBER CAMP FOLKS come forward.)

    LUMBERJACKS.
AND WE'RE PAPER COLLAR LUMBERJACKS,
WITH A BACKSAW ON OUR BACKS,
AND A TWO BIT TWO-BIT AXE,
    ALL.
COME TO LIVE IN SHANTY SHACKS,
COME TO CHANGE THE ALMANACS!
AND CONQUER THE LAND!

AND WE CAME TO CHANGE THE ALMANACS!
AND CONQUER THE LAND!

(The noon WHISTLE blows. [Music Cue #3A] As the lumber camp FOLKS disperse, NECKTIES bumps into the BLIND GIRL. HE mimes an apology and THEY have a brief conversation. Then HE leaves. It's clear the BLIND GIRL doesn't want him to go. MUSIC underscores.
LIGHTS focus on the BLIND GIRL Outside the General Store.)

VOICE OF SELENA'S MOTHER. *(As always, heard but unseen; perhaps the NARRATOR is standing at a distance from Selena, facing upstage.)* Selena, I told you to wait for me outside the General Store and not talk to anybody—most especially a lumberjack.

GIRL THAT HAS NO SEEING. *(Out front.)* But he came right up to me ... and asked if he could help me. He thought I was lost. I told him I was waiting for you. He seemed right nice, and didn't talk coarse like the other lumbermen. His voice was soft—almost like a gentleman. He said his name was Mr. Givens. I think he liked me.

VOICE OF SELENA'S MOTHER. And I think you live in a dream world. It's unhealthy for a child your age.

GIRL THAT HAS NO SEEING. But, Mother, I'm not a child anymore. And he was—

VOICE OF SELENA'S MOTHER. *(Overlapping Selena's line.)* Stop prattling on about nonsense. I won't indulge you. Not when we've got ten quarts of beans to can at home. Now, let's go, Selena.

(As the female NARRATOR impatiently escorts SELENA out, the scene dissolves to:)

The Forest Path and the Forest Cathedral

(NECKTIES walks through the forest picking wildflowers. Unknown to him, OPAL is following.)

OPAL. Hello.

NECKTIES. (*Quickly hiding the flowers.*) Oh, uh, howdy. I heard about you. Yer the new girl.

OPAL. And you are the man that wears gray neckties. That is my special name for you—for you are the only man here that wears a necktie ... Angel Father wore a necktie.

NECKTIES. I understand yer folks is gone away.

OPAL. (*Matter-of-factly.*) Yes. (*A new thought.*) What is that behind your back?

NECKTIES. What, this? Just a bunch a weeds.

OPAL. It's a bunch of fleurs.

NECKTIES. Ya mean, flowers.

OPAL. Somebody leaves fleurs just like those near the house of the thought-girl.

NECKTIES. Ya mean, the mill owner's daughter.

OPAL. Yes. And I know who *leaves* them.

NECKTIES. I was afraid ya might.

OPAL. It was the tree fairies.

NECKTIES. Who?

OPAL. The magic tree fairies.

NECKTIES. Oh ... Okay.

OPAL. They bring wishes. They always did, when Angel Father was with me.

(Pause.)

NECKTIES. (*A thought.*) Hey. I got this mail order wish book. (*Takes out a catalogue from his nap sack.*) If you was a tree fairy pickin' out a wish fer a little girl, what would ya choose? (*Thumbing through; points.*) A bottle a Dr. Harvey's Worm Elixir?

OPAL. (*Giggling.*) No.

NECKTIES. No? (*Turns a few pages.*) Okay ... hold on ... how 'bout ... a Luxury, galvanized, indoor bath tub?

OPAL. (*Giggling more.*) No.

NECKTIES. No? Well, what, then?

OPAL. (*Pointing.*) Colored pencils to write with.

NECKTIES. Okay. If I see any tree fairies, I'll tell 'em.

OPAL. That's just what Angel Father would do. Men that wear neckties are a *multiplication table* of comfort. (*Takes the catalogue and begins looking through it.*) Now, let's pick out a *wife*.

NECKTIES. A wife?

OPAL. Yes.

NECKTIES. Sears and Roebuck don't sell wives, Opal.

OPAL. Then how does you get one?

NECKTIES. Good question. Why d'ya ask?

OPAL. The Gossip Sisters said you needed a wife, and *I* is going to help you find one!

NECKTIES. (*Playfully; taking back the catalogue.*) Off with ya.

(*Just then, the THOUGHT-GIRL enters, holding one of the wildflower bouquets*
[*Music Cue #3B*])

THOUGHT-GIRL. (*Timidly.*) Oh, hello, Mr. Givens.

NECKTIES. (*Hiding the flowers quickly.*) Miss Ryden.

OPAL. Look. She found a bunch of fleurs, too!

NECKTIES. (*To OPAL.*) Git along, Opal.

THOUGHT-GIRL. I find bunches along the path outside my house nearly everyday. It must be the school children that leave them.

NECKTIES. Yup, I 'spose so.

OPAL. It wasn't the *school children.*

NECKTIES. Opal.

OPAL. It was the *tree fairies.*

THOUGHT-GIRL. (*Maternal; delighted by the child.*) The tree fairies? I see.

OPAL. And guess what else? I've been praying seven times a day for the angels to bring *you* a baby!

THOUGHT-GIRL. A baby?

OPAL. As soon as possible. The Gossip Sisters said an old maid like you should have a baby by now. So I'm going to help you get one!

(While SHE is still talking, NECKTIES picks her up and whisks her away.)

NECKTIES. Off with ya!

[Music Cue #3B]

(OPAL runs off.
Finding themselves alone, NECKTIES and the THOUGHT-GIRL feel awkward.)

THOUGHT-GIRL. Oh, I—uh—see you found a bunch of these "fleurs," too.

NECKTIES. Found 'em? Oh, uh, yup. Yup, I did. I found 'em.

[Music Cue #3C]

THOUGHT-GIRL. They're pretty.

NECKTIES. Uh, yeah ... And so's yer—

THOUGHT-GIRL. Uh—

NECKTIES. (*Turning away.*) No, I mean, yer, uh—

THOUGHT-GIRL. Uh—(*Flustered and nervous, SHE leaves quickly.*)

NECKTIES. (*Unaware she has left.*) What I mean is, I know yer used ta the finer things in life—like store-bought roses. Ya see, it ain't the school children that leaves these wild-flowers ... actually, truth ta tell, it's— (*HE turns and finds her gone. [MusicCue #4: SEARS AND ROEBUCK WEDDING BAND]*)
GO ON, WALK AWAY.

I'M A WASTE OF TIME.
CAN'T TAKE YOU TO A DIMESTORE,
'CAUSE I HAVEN'T GOT A DIME.

DREAMS ARE ALL I GOT
THAT'S NOT IN SHORT SUPPLY.
BUT, IF I PRINTED MONEY,
THEN, I KNOW JUST WHAT I'D BUY:

THAT SEARS AND ROEBUCK WEDDING BAND
ON PAGE ONE HUNDRED THREE.
GOLD ELECTRO-PLATED,
WITH A LIFETIME GUARANTEE.

THAT SEARS AND ROEBUCK WEDDING BAND
TO FLASH BEFORE YOUR EYES.
ONE IN JUST YOUR SIZE.

(HE looks through the catalogue.)

   NECKTIES.
WHAT I CAN'T AFFORD,
THAT'S WHAT YOU SHOULD HAVE.
LIKE, AN "ACME WONDER WASHER,"
OR "BONJOUR PARISIAN SALVE." (*Pronounced
  crudely as "bahn-djurr" with a hard j and lots of r.*)
PATENT LEATHER SHOES,
OR A PATENT-PENDING SIEVE.
AND THERE'S SOMETHING WITH ENGRAVING
I'D GIVE ANYTHING TO GIVE:

*(OPAL appears. SHE hides and spies on NECKTIES
  from a distance.)*

   NECKTIES. (*Turns to a dog-eared page.*)
THAT SEARS AND ROEBUCK WEDDING BAND
ON PAGE ONE HUNDRED THREE.
GOLD ELECTRO-PLATED,

WITH A LIFETIME GUARANTEE.

THAT SEARS AND ROEBUCK WEDDING BAND,
DELIVERED C.O.D.
JUST FOR YOU, FROM ME.

SEE, AS LONG AS I KNOW
NOTHING'S GONNA COME TRUE,
GUESS I MIGHT AS WELL GO
FOR THE TOP A THE LINE—
FOR A *DE*LUXE EDITION,
LIKE YOU,
AND THAT

(OPAL joins him.)

   NECKTIES AND OPAL.
SEARS AND ROEBUCK WEDDING BAND
ON PAGE ONE HUNDRED THREE.
GOLD ELECTRO-PLATED,
WITH A LIFETIME GUARANTEE.
   NECKTIES.
A FELLA NEEDS A DREAM TO DREAM,
ESPECIALLY IF HE'S POOR.
THAT'S THE THING
THAT CATALOGUES
AND PRETTY GIRLS
ARE FOR.

(LIGHTS fade.)

      SEQUENCE THREE — The Next Day

(The NARRATORS enter.
[Music Cue #4A])

NARRATORS.
FIND THE WAY TO MAKE EARTH GLAD,
AND EARTH APPROACHES HEAVEN.

And so, Opal set out on her quest to bring folks "joy-feels"—
   whether they wanted them or not—
   Getting a wife for the man that wears gray neckties,
   and a baby for the thought-girl,
   teaching the blind girl to see,
   and turning Peter Paul Rubens into a "gentleman pig."

The Lane to the School House

(OPAL crosses through with her school books tied together, leading Peter Paul Rubens.)

NARRATORS.
So, on the morning of today,
when the mamma wasn't looking,
Opal snuck Peter Paul Rubens out of the pigpen.
OPAL. Peter Paul Rubens, I am going to turn you into a gentleman pig—just like Pygmalion. You shall have a footbath and a christening. But first, you has got to have the proper education.
NARRATORS. So, she took him to school.

The School House

(OPAL leads the pig to the school house and ties him up outside.
The TEACHER is a comically frightening giant, towering over the children, who are played by the other NARRATORS. Their "school desks" are perhaps overturned crates and washtubs.)

NARRATORS.
She tied Peter Paul Rubens up just outside the school
house door,
    and told him to:
OPAL. (*To the pig.*) Stay here and pay attention.
TEACHER. (*Thundering voice.*) Opal ... You are
tardy again! *Why?*
OPAL. Because there was trouble in the chicken
coop. Henry VIII pecked Pope Pius VII on the head.

*(The CHILDREN snicker. Peter Paul Rubens
    GRUNTS—done, as usual, by one of the male
    NARRATORS. ALL look in the direction of the pig.)*

TEACHER. Opal ... There is a hog tied up outside!
Why?!
OPAL. Because he is too fat to sit at a desk.

(The CHILDREN laugh.)

TEACHER. At recess, you will take the pig home!
OPAL. (*To audience.*) The teacher looked straight
looks. And I went to my desk beside the recite bench.
(*SHE sits.*) Then, the teacher asked questions she had
wants to have answers for. She did ask:
TEACHER. (*Referring to a large—perhaps unseen—
chart with her pointer.*) What are the names of the animals
in this picture?

*(The CHILDREN raise their hands excitedly—all but
    BIG JUDD.)*

OPAL. She did call on Big Judd ... And Big Judd got
up in his *slow* way ... (*An oafish BOY lumbers to his
feet.*) And he did say ....
BIG JUDD. I don't know, teacher.

*(The CHILDREN laugh. BIG JUDD laughs, too. The
TEACHER whacks him with her ruler.)*

OPAL. Then, the teacher asked Lola the same
question. *(LOLA jumps up coyly.)* And Lola answered all
in one breath:
LOLA. *(Breathlessly; primly.)* That is a horse and a
donkey and a goat. *(Curtsying.)* Thank you. Thank you
very much. *(SHE sits.)*
OPAL. The teacher did beam delights all over Lola ...
Then it was, the teacher called *my* name.
TEACHER. *(Ominously.)* Opal ...
OPAL. *(Stands. To audience.)* I had anticipations the
teacher would beam delights all over me, too.
TEACHER. What are the names of the animals in
this picture? *(OPAL hesitates.)* Well? What are they?
OPAL. *(Pointing to each.)* A poisson ... a moulot ...
and a canard.

(The CHILDREN begin laughing.)

TEACHER. What did you say?
OPAL. They are a poisson, a moulot, and a canard.
TEACHER. They are called no such thing!

[Music Cue #4B]

OPAL. Yes they are! Angel Father said so!
TEACHER. Don't you be insolent with me, young
lady!
LOLA. Maybe she's talking in tongues!
BIG JUDD. Maybe she's just stupid!
TEACHER. Children!

*(LAUGHTER. JEERING. Ad-lib furor. We hear Peter
Paul Rubens SNORTING angrily.)*

OPAL. (*To the children.*) Stop laughing! (*To the pig.*) Oh, Peter Paul Rubens, make them stop laughing!

(*The pig charges into the classroom and chases the CHILDREN around and around, knocking over the school desks and causing pandemonium.*
TEACHER, CHILDREN, OPAL ad-lib commotion.
The chaotic scene whirls away behind OPAL as SHE runs with Peter Paul Rubens to:)

Sadie McKibben's Shanty

(*SADIE is scrubbing clothes on a washboard and tub. The shanty is strung with clotheslines of laundry. The GOSSIP SISTERS are there, bringing bundles of laundry.*
The MALE NARRATOR who provides the pig-noises observes the scene unobtrusively from the sidelines.)

OPAL. (*Overlapping the end of the commotion.*) Sadie McKibben! Sadie McKibben! Come, Peter Paul Rubens! Sadie McKibben! (*Etc.*)

GOSSIP SISTERS. (*To audience.*) It's that demented little girl—and she's got a hog!

SADIE. What's wrong, my child?

OPAL. Peter Paul Rubens was ex-spelled from school—because he needs a footbath and the mamma won't let me use the washtub. He wants to become a gentleman pig.

SADIE. (*Unfazed at having a pig in her kitchen.*) Does he, now?

OPAL. But the teacher shouted and the children all laughed at us.

SADIE. But, why?

OPAL. (*Still quite upset.*) Because we call things by names Angel Father taught me.

SADIE. Whatever do ye mean?

OPAL. (*Pointing to Sadie's boot.*) He called this une bottine.

(GOSSIP SISTERS gasp.)

OPAL. (*Pointing to the scrubbing board.*) And this, une planch a laver.

(GOSSIP SISTERS: bigger gasp.)

OPAL. (*Pointing to an apron on one of the GOSSIP SISTERS.*) And this, un tablier.
GOSSIP SISTERS. She's not coo-coo, she's possessed!
SADIE. Hush, the both of ye! I'll not have ye talk such nonsense of the child!
GOSSIP SISTERS. But, she's dangerous! She's a menace to the community!
SADIE. The only menace to the community I see is two tittle-tattle biddies with run-away tongues!
GOSSIP SISTERS. We came to have our laundry washed, not to be insulted!
SADIE. I'm happy to do both at no extra charge!
GOSSIP SISTERS. As you already have one foot in the poorhouse, we will remind you that we can take our business elsewhere.
SADIE. (*Throwing them their laundry.*) Here! Take yir dirty wash! It's yir mouths that need the scrubbin'!
GOSSIPS SISTERS. Well! (*Ad-libs: I never! She's addled-brained! Of all the nerve! We don't have to be insulted like this! Etc.*)

(A squeak comes from OPAL.)

GOSSIP SISTERS. (*Suddenly quiet.*) Why, listen! She's making a demonic squeaking sound!

*(More SQUEAKS. The GOSSIP SISTERS creep over to
OPAL cautiously.)*

OPAL. That's not me. That's my petite moulot.
GOSSIP SISTERS. Your what?
OPAL. (*Taking Felix from her pocket.*) My mouse.

*(GOSSIP SISTERS: a gasp, a shriek. THEY scurry out
screaming and swooning. Ad-lib commotion.
[Music Cue: #4C])*

SADIE. (*Laughing.*) They'll be back. They're lazy,
and I'm the only scrubwoman in town!
OPAL. (*Suddenly listening; concerned.*) Oh, Sadie
McKibben! Felix Mendelssohn is squeaking his *cheese*
squeak!
SADIE. Oh, and I've not a speck of cheese. Sadie's
poor as a church mouse herself.
OPAL. Felix Mendelssohn longs for cheese, just like
I long for Angel Mother and Father.
SADIE. Aye.
OPAL. The man in the boat said they went under the
deep water to stay. And the mamma says they is in
heaven.
SADIE. And so they are.
OPAL. She said they're never coming back, but she
is wrong. They will be back soon—for they said if I
found the way to make earth glad, I would be near them.
SADIE. And so you will—but not in the way ye
intend.
OPAL. But I have been trying real hard to make
people be glad.
SADIE. Not glad without. Glad within.
OPAL. I don't understand.
SADIE. Ye must find peace inside, my child. They're
not coming back.
OPAL. Yes they are! I know they are. I just don't
know how. (*OPAL pets the pig.*)

SADIE. Then, perhaps they will help ye understand. Perhaps they will return—in a special way.

OPAL. How?

SADIE. (*Mystically—as if seeing a vision. [Music Cue #5: SEARCH FOR A SIGN]*)
YE ASK FOR A WAY
YE MAY HEAR FROM BEYOND.
A WAY FOR THE LOST TO BE FOUND.
AYE, THERE'S A WAY.
A WAY WITHOUT WORDS.
IT'S LANGUAGE IS HERE ALL AROUND.

(Lively tempo. SADIE continues to scrub and hang laundry as SHE sings.)

SADIE.
YE MUST SEARCH FOR A SIGN.
AYE, SEARCH FOR A SIGN.
A TOKEN OF JOY SHALL ARISE.

THEY WILL SEND YE A SIGN.
OPAL.
WHAT SORT OF A SIGN?
SADIE.
A PROPHET OF HOPE IN DISGUISE.
OPAL. I don't understand.
SADIE. (*Taking OPAL on her knee.*)
IT MAY BE A COINPIECE
YE FIND IN YIR PURSE,
THOUGH EMPTY A MOMENT BEFORE.
OR A FLOWER YE PRESSED THAT FALLS FROM A
  BOOK,
WHEN LONELINESS KNOCKS AT YIR DOOR.

SADIE.	**OPAL.**
	AT YOUR DOOR.

THESE ARE
  CERTAINLY SIGNS.

AYE, WONDROUS
  SIGNS

                    THESE ARE
                      CERTAINLY SIGNS
                    WONDER-NESS SIGNS.

YE SEE WITH YIR
  HEART, NOT YIR
  EYES.

                    SEE WITH YOUR
                      HEART,
                    NOT YOUR EYES.

YE MUST SEARCH FOR
  A SIGN.
YIR CERTAIN TO SEE,
  BOTH.
IF SIMPLE ENOUGH TO BE WISE.
  SADIE. All right, Peter Paul Rubens. We're going to
make you a gentleman pig!

*(Throughout the following, SADIE cheers OPAL by
  giving the pig a scrub down with a rag.)*

  SADIE.
MY HUSBAND DEPARTED—
MAY GOD REST HIS SOUL—
BEFORE ONE AND ONE COULD MAKE THREE.

BUT I THINK, PERHAPS,
HE SENT ME A SIGN,
THE DAY THAT HE SENT YE TO ME.

*(Wrings out the smelly rag in the washtub, then hands it
  to OPAL, who continues to scrub the pig.)*

SO BE NOT BEDEVILED
WHEN DEVILS BEFALL,
NOR TROUBLED WHEN TROUBLES BESET.

IF ALL ARE ABOVE,
THEN KNOW ABOVE ALL:
'TIS NOTHING BUT FOLLY TO FRET.

SADIE.	**OPAL.**
	NEVER FRET.
SIMPLY SEARCH FOR A SIGN.	
	SIMPLY SEARCH FOR A SIGN. SEARCH FOR A SIGN.
A MYSTICAL, MAGICAL CLUE.	
	PETER PAUL RUBENS WILL, TOO.
YE MUST SEARCH FOR A SIGN DIVINE TO DIVINE,	

FOR SOMEWHERE OUT
  THERE IS A SIGN
THAT IS SEARCHING
  FOR YOU.	

	THERE'S A SIGN, THAT IS SEARCHING FOR YOU!

*(As the song ends, SADIE douses the pig with a washtub
full of imaginary water. SQUEALING. SPLASHING.
OPAL and SADIE embrace, laughing.
Suddenly, the MAMMA barges in, followed by the
GOSSIP SISTERS. [MUSIC CUE: #5A])*

THE MAMMA. *(Grabs OPAL.)* Opal! I told ya ta
stay away from that pig! *(SHE gives OPAL a spank.)*
SADIE. Mrs. Potter, please—

(Satisfied, the GOSSIP SISTERS leave.)

THE MAMMA. You was brung here ta help me out, but all you been is a *nui*sance! Do you know what a *nui*sance is!?

OPAL. I don't even know what an *old*-sance is.

THE MAMMA. *(Preparing to spank her again.)* Don't chu sass me, unless yer wearin' cast iron underpants!

SADIE. Mrs. Potter, stop! Ye mustn't lay hand to the child. I'll not let ye! *(OPAL hides behind SADIE, clinging to her skirt.)* If it's angry ye'll be, then be angry with me.

THE MAMMA. That can be arranged, seein' as Opal's always over here lollygaggin', while I'm back home, doin' my chores an' hers.

SADIE. 'Tis I'm to fault fir keepin' her from her chores. I get a wee lonely and she does bring a smile.

THE MAMMA. An' walkin' my prize pig around, so it gits skinny? That's yer fault, too?

SADIE. Perhaps I filled her head with silly notions. Sadie's full of foolish stories, as everyone knows.

THE MAMMA. Then there's the broken weddin' china, an' the washtub that floated down the river, an' the fifty tomato plants that was yanked up so their toes could git some air. Come ta think of it, Mrs. McKibben, you have got a lot ta answer for.

SADIE. It's only that I—

THE MAMMA. It's only that I got crops ta tend an' livestock ta raise an' a husband that comes around less than Labor Day. An' just when I thought I couldn't be happier, I git Helpful Hannah, here, ta feed an' clothe.

OPAL. I thought my name was Opal.

THE MAMMA. You hush up.

SADIE. Mrs. Potter, is that any way to—

THE MAMMA. You want 'er?

SADIE. What?

THE MAMMA. I said, ya want 'er?

OPAL. Please take me.

SADIE. (*To Mrs. Potter.*) Ye know I can barely keep myself.

THE MAMMA. Then you hush up, too. I don't need talk. I don't need advice. I need somebody sometime ta take the load off a me. Just once! I need somebody ta be there ta help me. Just once! That's what I need. (*Pause.*) I suspect you got clothes ta scrub. Come on, Opal. (*OPAL doesn't budge.*) Opal!

SADIE. (*To OPAL.*) Ye go and mind yir elders. (*For the mamma's benefit.*) They may not be wiser than ye, but they've been foolish a lot longer. (*SADIE leaves hesitantly.*)

THE MAMMA. When we git home, remind me ta spank you some more.

([Music Cue #5B]
The MAMMA exits angrily, leaving OPAL. The other NARRATORS enter to observe from the sides of the playing area.
The scene shifts to:)

Mrs. Potter's Lumber Shanty

(A NARRATOR hands OPAL her diary to write in. It is a stack of brown pages, made from butchers' paper and old sacks, and tied along the binding with string.)

OPAL. (*Writing; speaking at a normal rate of speed.*) Dear Angel Mother and Father ... There is *bumps* on the mamma's temper. She said I was a new-sance. That's something bad ... Please come back to me real soon.

(By now, it is NIGHT.
There is a CRASH outside. GRUNTING. SQUEALING. Peter Paul Rubens waddles into the barnyard.

*OPAL checks to see that the MAMMA isn't watching,
then sneaks out the window to:)*

The Barnyard

(A pool of LIGHT establishes the pig's location.)

OPAL. *(To the pig.)* The teacher said you was a "new-sance." I'm a "newsance," too. But, don't be sad, Peter Paul Rubens. I need you to help me search for a sign. We shall make earth glad together. And, one day, the teacher will say: *(In the teacher's voice.)* "Why, Peter Paul Rubens, what a *proper gentleman pig* you have become." And then, I shall take you to the Louvre Museum, and show you all the pictures you painted. *(HE snorts.)* But, first, you must have your christening.

[Music Cue #6: LITTLE LAMB]

NARRATORS.
And she christened him,
singing a lullaby poem by William Blake—
a lullaby she used to hear each night.
OPAL.
LITTLE LAMB, WHO MADE THEE?
DOST THOU KNOW WHO MADE THEE?

GAVE THEE LIFE AND BID THEE FEED,
BY THE STREAM AND O'RE THE MEAD.
                    NARRATORS.
    OPAL.   OOOH … *(Etc.)*
GAVE THEE CLOTHING OF DELIGHT,
SOFTEST CLOTHING, WOOLY BRIGHT
GAVE THEE SUCH A TENDER VOICE,
MAKING ALL THE VALES REJOICE.
    OPAL. *(Alone.)*
LITTLE LAMB, WHO MADE THEE?
DOST THOU KNOW WHO MADE THEE?

(A NARRATOR hands OPAL a watering can. OPAL reaches in and sprinkles water on the pig's head. HE squeals.)

OPAL.
LITTLE LAMB, I'LL TELL THEE.

HE IS CALLED BY THY NAME,
FOR HE CALLS HIMSELF A LAMB:
    OPAL and NARRATORS.
HE IS MEEK AND HE IS MILD,
HE BECAME A LITTLE CHILD:
I A CHILD AND THOU A LAMB,
WE ARE CALLED BY HIS NAME.
    OPAL.
LITTLE LAMB, GOD BLESS THEE.
LITTLE LAMB, GOD BLESS THEE.

(The pig rolls over and wiggles in the mud, SNORTING. OPAL kneels beside him.)

OPAL. *(A realization.)* Why, Peter Paul Rubens! *I* know why you roll in the mud: You want to get *roots*, and grow into a beautiful *flower*.

(SHE kisses her hand and touches his head. He GRUNTS. Worried the MAMMA will hear, SHE shushes him. LIGHTS fade.)

SEQUENCE FOUR — Fall

The Ranch House Social

([Music Cue #7: NIGHT OF SHOOTING STARS]

Lanterns; streamers; harvest decorations; fall colors;
   magical hoedown MUSIC; HOOTS and HOLLERS.
The entire lumber camp is there—including OPAL, the
   MAMMA, NECKTIES, SADIE, the THOUGHT-
   GIRL, and the GIRL THAT HAS NO SEEING.
   PEOPLE congregate and finish decorating, waiting for
   the dance to begin.)

SQUARE DANCE CALLER. Welcome, one and
all, to the Harvest-time Social! Everybody find yerself a
partner.

(OPAL runs up to the THOUGHT-GIRL, who is holding
   a baby. The GOSSIP SISTERS are nearby, also
   minding babies.)

OPAL. Why, look! The angels have brought you the
baby I've been praying for you to have. That was fast!
   THOUGHT-GIRL. No, dear. This isn't my baby. I
don't have one.
   OPAL. You will when I get through! (*SHE goes to*
SADIE.)
   SQUARE DANCE CALLER. Shanty boys on my
left. Eligible ladies on my right. I guarantee you'll meet
your sweetheart tonight!
   GOSSIP SISTERS. (*To the THOUGHT-GIRL,.)*
Go out and dance, Miss Ryden. You heard what he said.
He guarantees you'll meet your sweetheart tonight.
   THOUGHT-GIRL. But, I'm minding the babies.
   GOSSIP SISTERS. (*Taking her baby.*) We'll mind
the babies. You mind the men.

(At other side of the dance floor:)

GENERAL STORE OWNER. (*Nudging NECK-*
TIES.) Go on, Andrew. Ask 'er ta dance.
   ANDREW. Who, me?

GENERAL STORE OWNER. Everybody knows ya want to. Everybody but her, that is.

(THE GENERAL STORE OWNER shoves NECKTIES across the dance floor to the THOUGHT-GIRL.)

NECKTIES. Uh, Miss Ryden—
GOSSIP SISTERS. (*Pushing the THOUGHT-GIRL into Neckties' arms.*) She'd *love* to.

(NECKTIES and the THOUGHT-GIRL are mortified. THEY rush to opposite sides of the dance floor as lively MUSIC begins.
OPAL dances with SADIE at one side of the stage. The BLIND GIRL sits in a chair downstage to one side, singing along and trying to sense the motion of the dance.
This number is about the collision of two story lines: NECKTIES/ THOUGHT-GIRL and NECKTIES/ BLIND GIRL.
As EVERYONE sings, the SQUARE DANCE CALLER—perhaps playing a fiddle—goes around coaxing people onto the dance floor. THEY resist shyly at first, but, little by little, a square dance ensues.)

ALL.
IT'S THE HARVEST ONCE-A-YEAR JAMBOREE,
IT'S THE ONCE-A-YEAR YOUR FANCY IS FREE.
ALL THE BEAUS ARE WEARING
BOW-TIES,
AND THEY'RE FEELIN' SHY AS
SHOO-FLIES,
BUT THEY'RE QUITE A SIGHT FOR
SORE EYES
TO SEE.
HEAR THE FIDDLE PLAYER SCRATCHIN' HIS
   BOW,

WITH A FIDDLE-DIDDLE-DIDDLE-LEE-DOE.

(The CALLER makes reference to the GOSSIP SISTERS. THEY don't appreciate it.)

ALL THE OLD MAIDS GOSSIP AND STARE,

(Making reference to OPAL and SADIE—who are doing a lively dance by now.)

WHILE THE YOUNG MAIDS FLY THROUGH
THE AIR,
AND THE RAFTERS RATTLE,
LIKE JER-
ICHO.

(Little by little, the mill town FOLKS begin joining in. Laughter. Hoots. Hollers. Clapping and improvised folk instruments. A rowdy, spontaneous-looking dance begins—semi-organized Virginia reels, promenades, do-si-do's, etc.)

IT'S A NIGHT OF SHOOTING STARS,
WHEN THEY RICOCHET ABOVE.
IT'S NIGHT FOR MAKING WISHES,
AND A NIGHT TO FALL IN LOVE.

(OPAL leaves SADIE and goes to the BLIND GIRL. Throughout the following, OPAL mimes a conversation with the BLIND GIRL, trying to coax her out of her chair and onto the dance floor.)

SO, DON'T LET YOUR "GET-UP" GET UP AND GO,
'CAUSE THE NIGHT IS YOUNG, AND, YOU
   NEVER KNOW—
EVERY LAD MAY FIND HIM
HIS GAL,
AND ANOTHER GAL FOR

HIS PAL, HERE AMONG THE RUFFLES
AND CAL-
ICO.

IT'S A NIGHT OF SHOOTING STARS,
WHEN THEY RICOCHET ABOVE.
IT'S A NIGHT FOR MAKING WISHES,
AND A NIGHT TO FALL IN LOVE.

*(Lines of women. Lines of men. Two by two, couples
are formed. Suddenly, NECKTIES and the
THOUGHT-GIRL find themselves pushed out into the
center of the dance floor, face to face.)*

GENERAL STORE OWNER. Go on, Andrew.
Give 'er a whirl!

*(MILL TOWN FOLKS: Whistles. Hoots. And ad-libs of
encouragement—"Go on." "She don't bite." "Dance,
you two." etc.*
*NECKTIES reaches out. The THOUGHT-GIRL takes
his hand. At first unsteadily, THEY begin to dance.*
*Meanwhile, OPAL is teaching the BLIND GIRL a
minuet. THEY begin whirling together—slowly, at
first, growing faster and faster and more reckless.)*

ALL.
IT'S A NIGHT OF SHOOTING STARS,
WHEN THEY RICOCHET ABOVE.
IT'S A NIGHT FOR MAKING WISHES,
AND A NIGHT TO FALL IN LOVE.

IT'S A NIGHT OF SHOOTING STARS,
THOUGH THEY ONLY SHINE 'TIL DAWN.

BUT, IF YOU SHOULD MEET YOUR SWEET-
HEART,
THEN THE SHOOTING STARS GO ON

AND—

*(Suddenly, the BLIND GIRL collides with NECKTIES.
SHE falls to the floor. The MUSIC stops. The mill
town FOLKS gather around. NECKTIES and the
THOUGHT-GIRL help SELENA to her feet. The
MAMMA spanks OPAL and pulls her aside.)*

MILL TOWN FOLKS. (*Ad-lib commotion.*) Are
you all right, Selena? ... She's the blind girl ... It was
that foreign girl's fault ... (*Etc.*)
NECKTIES. Lemme help ya, Selena.
GIRL THAT HAS NO SEEING. (*Deeply
embarrassed.*) I'm perfectly fine, thank you.
THOUGHT-GIRL. Shall I get the doctor?
GIRL THAT HAS NO SEEING. Don't fuss,
please. Just lead me back to my chair. My mother will be
back soon.
NECKTIES. (*With a glance towards the
THOUGHT-GIRL.*) Sure, Selena. Lemme help ya.

*(The THOUGHT-GIRL goes back to minding the baby.
NECKTIES takes SELENA back to her chair.)*

GIRL THAT HAS NO SEEING. Tell everyone
to go on dancing.
NECKTIES. You heard what she said. Go on.

*(The MILL TOWN FOLKS back away. THEY converse
among themselves and gradually disperse.
[Music Cue #7A])*

NECKTIES. I'll just sit with ya 'til—
GIRL THAT HAS NO SEEING. That's all right,
Mr. Givens.
NECKTIES. Oh, ya remember me.
GIRL THAT HAS NO SEEING. You don't have
to stay.

NECKTIES. But, I'd like to.

GIRL THAT HAS NO SEEING. I'm certain you'd much rather be dancing with the others.

NECKTIES. No, not me. I don't think my partner would wanna dance with me again, anyway. Not that I blame 'er. I got these two feet that don't git along with each other. I make a spectacle when I try ta dance.

GIRL THAT HAS NO SEEING. Me too.

NECKTIES. I'm sorry, Selena. I didn't mean—

GIRL THAT HAS NO SEEING. Are they watching?

NECKTIES. Who?

GIRL THAT HAS NO SEEING. The other folks. Are they all looking at me?

NECKTIES. No, Selena. Nobody's lookin'.

GIRL THAT HAS NO SEEING. I'm only glad mamma wasn't here to see. She'd never let me forget it. Sit in the corner. That's your place, she said. It makes folks uneasy if you try to socialize, she said.

NECKTIES. Well, now, that ain't true. Not a bit.

GIRL THAT HAS NO SEEING. That's nice of you to say.

NECKTIES. I mean it. Yer fine company.

GIRL THAT HAS NO SEEING. Thank you.

NECKTIES. Yer perty. Yer bright. An' yer easy ta talk to—which is a good thing fer a tongue-tied fella, like me.

GIRL THAT HAS NO SEEING. Thank you, Mr. Givens. You're easy to talk to, too.

NECKTIES. (*Pause.*) I'll go git yer mamma fer ya.

GIRL THAT HAS NO SEEING. But, Mr. Givens, I—

(HE is gone.
OPAL comes to SELENA.)

OPAL. You had a big fall-down.

GIRL THAT HAS NO SEEING. Yes, I did.

OPAL. I have thinks you cannot see because your glasses is painted black.

GIRL THAT HAS NO SEEING. I'm blind, Opal. That means I can't see.

OPAL. Then, why must you wear glasses?

GIRL THAT HAS NO SEEING. The glasses aren't for *my* eyes. They're for everyone else's eyes.

[MUSIC CUE #7B]

OPAL. Maybe when I'm grown-up, that will make sense. I only know that if potatoes have eyes, and they can see what goes on in the darkness underground, then you can see, too.

(The MAMMA comes to OPAL.)

THE MAMMA. Opal. I'm goin' home early. I got somethin' that needs to be done. You can do what chu want for a little while. *(The MAMMA exits.)*

OPAL. *(Reacts; puzzled.)* That's something I never heard the mamma say before. *(A thought.)* Do you want to go on an exploration trip?

GIRL THAT HAS NO SEEING. What for?

OPAL. So I can teach you to see without eyes!

(OPAL takes SELENA by the hand and whisks her out into the night. The ranch house vanishes behind them as THEY enter:)

The Forest

(A cold wind whooshes through the trees. ANIMALS and BIRDS call. Night CRICKETS chirp. The NARRATORS intone the mystical "Earth Voices" theme.
OPAL pulls the BLIND GIRL deeper and deeper into the dark, mysterious forest.)

THE VOICE OF SELENA'S MOTHER. (*Calling from a great distance; unseen throughout.*) Seleeeeenaaaaa!

(*The NARRATOR providing the mother's voice is onstage—facing upstage or away from SELENA.*)

GIRL THAT HAS NO SEEING. (*Frightened.*) Opal, where are you taking me?!
OPAL. (*Through much of this scene, in a voice of wonderment and mystery.*) To my forest cathedral.
SELENA'S MOTHER. Seleeeenaaaa!
GIRL THAT HAS NO SEEING. That's my mother. She's worried. She never lets me wander off alone.
OPAL. But, we aren't alone. Me and Michael Angelo are going to teach you to see without eyes!
GIRL THAT HAS NO SEEING. Who's that? Is someone else here?

(*THEY arrive at:*)

The Forest Cathedral

(*A lush vault of towering pines; majestic shafts of moonlight filter down through pine branches.*
The NARRATORS form themselves into a fir tree— perhaps by holding branches and standing on graduated crates and barrels.)

OPAL. Michael Angelo is a fir tree. His soul is very old and wise. (Listens suddenly.) *Listen! He is speaking to us! He wants to give you one of his arms—to use as a feeling stick.* (OPAL goes to break off a branch.)
GIRL THAT HAS NO SEEING. (*Confused and scared.*) His arm?

OPAL. (*Deep voice.*) "Take my arm," he says, "trust me and I shall guide you." (*OPAL snaps off the branch.*)

GIRL THAT HAS NO SEEING. (*Alarmed.*) Opal, what are you doing? I don't want —(*OPAL puts the branch in her hand. Relief; a small, tense laugh.*) Oh ... It's only a branch. A walking stick.

OPAL. A *feeling* stick. To have *sees* by *feels*. To go adventuring by yourself.

GIRL THAT HAS NO SEEING. Mother would never let me do that.

OPAL. The mamma never does, neither. But tonight must be a special night.

SELENA'S MOTHER. Seleeeeenaaaa!

GIRL THAT HAS NO SEEING. Show me how to use this.

OPAL. (*Guiding her hand.*) Like this ... side to side ... inch by inch ... like a caterpillar making "s" 's along the path. (*OPAL lets go. SELENA continues on her own.*) Soon you shall come to the forest alone whenever you wish—to drink in inspirations.

GIRL THAT HAS NO SEEING. (*Amazed at her ability.*) Yes. Yes, I can do this.

(*OPAL kneels and takes a small candle from her apron pocket and lights it.*)

OPAL. (*Singing a Gregorian chant; solemnly.*)
GLORIA DOMINE,
GLORIA DOMINE.

GIRL THAT HAS NO SEEING. What are you doing?

OPAL. Lighting a candle of hope, as Angel Father did when he took me to the cathedral in the far-away lands. He said the flame was full of gladness and hope.

GIRL THAT HAS NO SEEING. (*Comes to OPAL, using the stick; kneels beside her.*) Oh, Opal ... a long time ago—when I was your age—I imagined wonderful things, like you. I heard voices. I lit candles in the dark ... But, that was before the blind fever came on me ... and everything was over before it began.

OPAL. What can you see when you cannot see?

GIRL THAT HAS NO SEEING. You see nothings, Opal. It's always midnight. It's always very, very black.

OPAL. Oh.

[Music Cue #8: OPAL]

GIRL THAT HAS NO SEEING. Opal ... tell me something ... what color are Mr. Givens' eyes?

OPAL. Sky color.

GIRL THAT HAS NO SEEING. I thought so ... I thought so ...
OPAL,
BEFORE I GREW,
I SAW
A CHILD LIKE YOU
INSIDE A LOOKING GLASS.
AND SHE WAS ME, REVERSED.

OPAL,
MY OTHER HALF
KNEW HOW
TO PLAY AND LAUGH.
SHE KNEW THE SECRET GAMES
WE ONLY KNOW AT FIRST.

(SELENA moves away, lost in memory.)

SHE SAW YOUR WORLD,
THAT WORLD OF HOPE AND SURPRISE,
FULL OF DRAGONS AND CASTLES,
AND FAIRY QUEENS AND VASSALS,
AND A PRINCE
WITH SKY-COLORED EYES.

OPAL,
WHAT FRIENDS WE WERE,
'TIL I
LOST SIGHT OF HER.
WHEN LAST I SAW MYSELF,
SHE'S WHO I USED TO BE.

OPAL,
IF YOU SHOULD KNOW
WHERE OLD
REFLECTIONS GO,
HELP ME LOOK
THROUGH THAT LOOKING-GLASS SEA,
FOR THAT LONG LOST OPAL
IN ME.

*(The MUSIC swells. OPAL comes to SELENA and
hands her the candle. SELENA blows it out.
Suddenly, we hear an animal's distant, piteous
SQUEAL—as created by the NARRATORS.)*

[Music Cue #8A]

OPAL. (*Alarmed.*) That was Peter Paul Rubens! He
needs me!
GIRL THAT HAS NO SEEING. Go, Opal. I can
find my way myself.

*(The other NARRATORS join in the squealing sound,
making a nightmarish din.
The scene dissolves cinematically, as we watch OPAL
running breathlessly through the forest—perhaps
circling the stage—to:)*

The Barnyard

*(There, in the Potter's barnyard, we see the MAMMA
wiping a large butcher's knife on her apron. Peter Paul*

*Rubens lies on the ground dying—defined, as before,
by a pool of LIGHT.
OPAL runs in and halts suddenly—aghast.
OPAL screams.)*

THE MAMMA. I warned ya from the start—the hogs is all I got ta sell. Otherwise, we both starve.
OPAL. (*Running to the pig.*) Noooo!

*(SHE kneels on the ground and cradles the pig's head in
her lap. The MAMMA exits. The NARRATORS watch
from the surrounding shadows.
We hear the MUSIC BOX theme playing—slowing down
little by little. Peter Paul Rubens makes a low,
WHEEZING sound.)*

OPAL. Oh, Peter Paul Rubens, you are becoming empty.
NARRATORS.
LITTLE LAMB, WHO MADE THEE?
DOST THOU KNOW WHO MADE THEE?

GAVE THEE LIFE ...

*(The MUSIC BOX slows to a stop. Peter Paul Rubens
dies. The NARRATORS create the sound of a distant,
icy WIND rising and falling.)*

OPAL. You *are* empty. (*Pause.*) Your soul is gone away, like Angel Mother and Father. (*Pause.*) I shall find where souls go, Peter Paul Rubens, so that no one shall ever go away again. (*Pause; very slowly.*) I shall find ... your ... soul.

*(LIGHTS dim very slowly. The WIND fades. Long
BLACKOUT.)*

SEQUENCE FIVE — Late Winter

The Lumber Camp

[Music Cue #9: TO CONQUER THE LAND (Reprise)]

(SUNRISE. We see the LUMBER CAMP FOLKS in silhouette. The LIGHTS come up slowly throughout the following.)

TWO MALE NARRATORS.
(Singly.)
AND WE RISE,
AND WE WORK,
(Together.)
IN THE ICY WINTER DAWN.
　　TWO FEMALE NARRATORS.
(Singly.)
AND WE CHOP,
AND WE CLEAR
(Together.)
FOR A YEAR, AND THEN MOVE ON.
　　ALL NARRATORS.
AND WE ...

(Activity begins. FULL CAST enters. Rhythmic work movements. The weather is cold and harsh. We see the LUMBER CAMP FOLKS swathed in tattered coats and scarves. Some mime huddling before a fire, trying to stay warm.)

ALL. *(But OPAL.)*
... CAME TO TAME THE LAST FRONTIER,
LEAVING ALL THAT'S NEAR AND DEAR,
CAME THIS WAY TO PIONEER,
AND CONQUER THE LAND!

LUMBERJACKS.	**WOMEN.**
AND WE HACK,	
	AND WE SCRUB,
AND WE HEW,	
	AND WE SCRAPE,
AND WE TETHER, TIE, AND SAW.	
	AND SAW.
AND WE GRIND,	
	AND WE STRAIN,
AND WE CLAMP,	
	AND WE POUND,
AND WE WORK ALL.	
OUR FINGERS RAW.	

AND WE CAME TO TAME HE LAST FRONTIER,
CAME TO LIVE WITH STRANGERS HERE,
CAME TO CLEAR AND PIONEER,
AND CONQUER THE LAND!

(THEY freeze. LIGHTS focus on OPAL, who is writing in her diary.)

OPAL. Dear Angel Mother and Father ... the glad song in my heart plays slower and slower, now that Peter Paul Rubens is gone away. *(SHE leaves her diary and comes downstage. Out front.)* The mamma says his soul is gone for good. But, I don't believe her—for, if he is gone for good, then maybe so are you. *(SHE runs up to a lumberjack.)* Do you know where the soul of Peter Paul Rubens is?

LUMBERJACK. *(Harshly.)* Go away.

OPAL. *(SHE runs up to the GOSSIP SISTERS.)* Have you seen the soul of a pig?

GOSSIP SISTERS. *(Gesturing.)* Shoo!

NECKTIES. (*Comes to OPAL bringing her colored pencils.*) Hey, will ya look at this? Them tree fairies brought ya more colored pencils.

OPAL. (*Trying to be happy.*) Oh.

NECKTIES. Opal, ya gotta stop singin' that same sad song.

OPAL. But, the soul of Peter Paul Rubens is gone away. I must find it, or it shall be lost forever.

NECKTIES. Where's that happy little girl I used ta know, huh? She's the one that's gone away.

(*HE rejoins the ensemble. SADIE MCKIBBEN comes to OPAL.*)

OPAL. (*Out front.*) Sadie McKibben said you would send me ...

SADIE. (*To OPAL.*) A sign. A secret sign ...

(*SADIE stands behind OPAL with her hand on Opal's shoulder.*)

OPAL. (*Out front.*) ... to teach me how you can be near, though you be far .... So, if you can open the gates of heaven just once, show me where things go that are gone for good. Help me find the soul of my pig—or I have thinks I shall never, never be able to make earth glad.

SHOW ME WHERE HIS SOUL IS,
NOW THAT HE'S NOT MINE.
MOTHER,
FATHER,
THAT WILL BE YOUR SIGN.
THAT WILL BE YOUR *SIGN*.

(*The MAMMA appears suddenly.*)

THE MAMMA. (*Harshly.*) Opal! There's chores ta do!

(*With an angry look at SADIE, MRS. POTTER yanks OPAL away and hands her a broom. OPAL sweeps.*)

ALL. (*But OPAL.*)
AND WE RISE,
AND WE WORK,
IN THE BITING WINTER AIR.

(*The OTHERS freeze.*)

OPAL. (*Out front.*)
AND I WAIT,
AND I HOPE,
AND I WONDER IF YOU'RE THERE.

(*Activity resumes.*)

LUMBERJACKS.
AND WE'RE PAPER COLLAR LUMBERJACKS,
WITH A BACKSAW ON OUR BACKS,
AND A TWO BIT TWO-BIT AXE,
    ALL. (*But OPAL.*)
COME TO LIVE IN SHANTY SHACKS,
COME TO CHANGE THE ALMANACS,
AND CONQUER THE LAND!

AND WE CAME TO CHANGE THE ALMANACS,
AND CONQUER THE LAND!

(*LIGHTS cross fade, showing a change of season.*)

SEQUENCE SIX — Spring

The Forest Path

[Music Cue #10: SOMEONE]

(As the LUMBER CAMP FOLKS disperse, NECKTIES looks around to make sure no one is watching, then secretly lays a bunch of wildflowers along the path.)

NARRATORS.
Spring came.
And, once more, the thought-girl began finding bunches of wildflowers
left along the path outside her home.

(Unknown to NECKTIES, the THOUGHT-GIRL has seen him. After HE leaves, SHE fetches the flowers. LIGHTS focus in on the thought-girl.)

THE THOUGHT-GIRL (*Out front; to herself.*)
I HAVE A SOMEONE
DREAMING OF ME,
LEAVING DAISIES EACH DAY.

SOMEONE WHO IS TIMID, AND YET UNDE-
TERRED.
TELLING ME HE CARES,
WITHOUT SAYING A WORD.

MY SECRET
SOMEONE IMAGINES
NO ONE CAN SEE
ALL HE'S UNABLE TO SAY.

IF HE
ONLY
TOLD ME, HE'D SEE

I HAVE A SOMEONE
AND SO DOES HE.

The Homes of the Thought-Girl and the Girl That Has No Seeing

THOUGHT-GIRL. You see, Father, he's a lumberjack ...

(A LIGHT comes up on SELENA, standing at another part of the stage. SHE and the THOUGHT-GIRL are in their own separate worlds.)

G.T.H.N.S. (*Out front; she and the THOUGHT-GIRL speak simultaneously.*)

THOUGHT-GIRL.
He's thoughtful and quiet and kind. And he leaves me flowers along the path every day.

Remember, Mother? I met him outside the General Store last fall. No, he hasn't exactly said so in so many words. But,

BOTH.
I DON'T NEED TO HEAR
WHAT I ALREADY KNOW ...

THOUGHT-GIRL.	**G.T.H.N.S.**
MY SECRET	INSIDE ME.
SOMEONE IMAGINES	I KNOW, FINALLY,
NO ONE CAN SEE	I HAVE A SOMEONE,
ALL HE'S UNABLE TO	MOTHER, STOP
SAY.	LAUGHING.
	I KNOW THAT
	HE CARES FOR
	ME, IN HIS
	OWN WAY.
IF HE	SOMEDAY,
ONLY	YOU'LL SEE.
TOLD ME, HE'D SEE,	

BOTH.
I HAVE A SOMEONE
AND SO DOES HE.
   GIRL THAT HAS NO SEEING. (*In tears.*) I
don't care what you say, Mother.
   THOUGHT-GIRL.
I'VE ALWAYS KNOWN—
   GIRL-THAT HAS NO SEEING. It's true.
   BOTH.
I HAVE A SOMEONE,
WHO'S MINE
ALONE.

(*LIGHTS fade.*)

SEQUENCE SEVEN — Summer

Mrs. Potter's Shanty

(*The MAMMA enters carrying a heavy crate. As SHE
   bangs it down on the floor, a locket on a necklace falls
   out from under her blouse. SHE automatically starts to
   put it back, but then stops and opens the locket.
   LIGHTS focus down on her.*
[*Music Cue #10A*])

   THE MAMMA.
YOU'D A BEEN PERTY,
PERTY AS SIN.
CAN'T HELP BUT THINK, EVERYTHING THAT
   MIGHTA BEEN.

WE'D A BEEN HAPPY,
IF YOU'D A GROWN,
US AN' YOUR PA—
'STEAD WHICH, I END UP ...

WHY DOES IT SEEM
LIKE I ALWAYS END UP
ALONE?

(OPAL enters carrying her diary. Seeing the MAMMA, SHE hides it quickly in her apron pocket.)

THE MAMMA. *(Putting the locket away.)* You got them chores done, yet?
OPAL. What chores?
THE MAMMA. Criminy! *(Pronounced "crime-in-nee.")* With you ta help, it only takes me twice as long. Why was I ever fool enough ta name ya after Opal? *She* was a good lil' girl. She tried ta please me.

(The MAMMA begins taking various metal parts from the crate. Throughout the following, SHE assembles a meat grinder.)

OPAL. *Who* was good?
THE MAMMA. Never mind.
OPAL. *What* little girl?
THE MAMMA. *(Exasperated.)* Opal. *(Pause.)* My girl.
OPAL. Where is she?
THE MAMMA. She's dead.
OPAL. When will she be back?
THE MAMMA. She's gone fer good.
OPAL. Like Angel Mother and Father?
THE MAMMA. Yup.
OPAL. And Peter Paul Rubens?
THE MAMMA. Yeah.
OPAL. Maybe they know one another.
THE MAMMA. *(Exploding.)* Girl, when are you gonna understand the way things is?! When ya gonna learn that—? *(SHE chokes back a sob.)*

OPAL. What is wrong? You look like you is going to have cry feels ... I did not know you even could ... Don't be sad ... She's not gone away for good. You just have needs for a sign.

THE MAMMA. Oh, hush! Yer always babblin'. An' what's worse is, I'm startin' ta listen! If there's one thing you've gotten better at, it's wastin' my time.

([Music Cue #10B]
SHE finishes assembling the meat grinder. The NARRATORS enter to observe the scene.)

THE MAMMA. Now, come here an' listen with both ears. This is called a *grinder* ... Ya put the meat in this end ... ya turn the handle, like so ... an' it comes out here.

(As SHE turns the handle, the grinder makes a rusty sounding SQUEAK—perhaps created by a narrator with a sound effect apparatus. In addition, the NARRATORS intone a painful, deathly moaning— distant, tortured cries that rise higher as the grinder handled is turned faster.)

THE MAMMA. (*Finishing.*) Now, you do it.

(Throughout the following, the LIGHTING causes the grinder to become more and more menacing. The scene becomes ever more nightmarish.)

OPAL. (*Upset and fearful.*) No. The grinder has a squeaky voice.

THE MAMMA. Grind the sausage.

OPAL. No. (*Near tears.*) I don't want to!

THE MAMMA. (*Grabbing OPAL; dragging her to the grinder and forcing her to grind.*) I don't care what chu want. I got a heap a chores ta do, an' five pounds a sausage that'll spoil 'less you grind it. Now, do as I say! Go on!

(*As OPAL and the MAMMA make the grinder handle go around faster and faster, the grinder takes on a life of its own. Round and round goes the handle. More squeals and squeaks. The NARRATORS' death cries rise higher and higher.*)

OPAL. (*Finally bursting into tears.*) No! No! I won't! I won't! (*OPAL runs out.*)
THE MAMMA. Come back here! I'll whup you! Come back here!

(*OPAL circles the playing area and runs through the forest to:*)

The Forest Cathedral

NARRATORS. (*To audience.*)
Opal ran to the forest cathedral,
to talk things over with Michael Angelo, the fir tree.

(*OPAL runs to Michael Angelo the fir tree—portrayed, as before, by the NARRATORS.*)

OPAL. (*Calling as she runs to him.*) Oh, Michael Angelo! (*To the tree.*) The mamma made me to grind sausage. And every time I made turns on the handle, I could hear the little pain squeal of Peter Paul Rubens. (*Listens.*) What did you say? (*Listens.*) Yes ... That's true ... I knew you would know the right thing to say. Let me climb up into your arms.

(*SHE climbs up into the tree. The NARRATORS lift her up to the top, where a MALE NARRATOR holds her in his arms. They are somewhat BACKLIT, suggesting she is high up in the fir tree's branches.*)

NARRATORS.
And she climbed up into his branches,
where the world looks like a dollhouse,
and very big problems seem much, much smaller.
OPAL. (*To the tree.*) It is such a comfort to snuggle
in your strong arms ... You have such an understanding
soul. (*SHE hugs him.*) Why, when I hug you, I can hear
your sap going up! It sounds like springtime.

(*NECKTIES enters leading SELENA by the arm.*)

NARRATORS.
And that was when she overheard the man that wears
gray neckties,
leading the blind girl home through the forest.
OPAL. Look, Michael Angelo. The girl that has no
seeing is out on explores.
NECKTIES. (*To SELENA.*) This woods is a
dangerous place for someone like you.
GIRL THAT HAS NO SEEING. (*Playing the
romantic subtext throughout.*) Really?
NECKTIES. The woods is a tinder box this time a
year. An' we're cuttin' trees. Well, who knows what
could happen.
GIRL THAT HAS NO SEEING. I appreciate
your concern. It means a lot.
NECKTIES. I can't imagine why yer folks just let a
youngin' like you wander off alone, like that.
GIRL THAT HAS NO SEEING. They don't.
But, I've got a mind of my own, Mr. Givens, and it's
high time I start using it.
NECKTIES. Ain't chu afraid?
GIRL THAT HAS NO SEEING. Not really. The
forest looks the same to me as our parlour. What you
can't see, can't scare you.
NECKTIES. You got spunk, that's fer sure.
GIRL THAT HAS NO SEEING. Is that good?

NECKTIES. I'll say. Maybe if I had some a yer spunk, I wouldn't always be so tongue-tied all over the place.

GIRL THAT HAS NO SEEING. I don't think you're tongue-tied.

NECKTIES. No, not around you. Yer easy ta talk to. But at the ranch house socials or such ... my mouth runs outa words.

GIRL THAT HAS NO SEEING. Oh, I don't know, Mr. Givens. Sometimes, you don't even need words. Sometimes, a person just knows.

NECKTIES. (*Pause.*) Let's git chu back home. I suspect you wanna pay a visit on Elsie Fairchild.

GIRL THAT HAS NO SEEING. What for?

NECKTIES. Ain't chu heard?

GIRL THAT HAS NO SEEING. No, what?

NECKTIES. That baby finally come ta Elsie an' her husband last night. (*With a little laugh.*) Come on.

(*HE pulls her off playfully—almost seeming like boyfriend and girlfriend. Ad-lib good humor and laughter as THEY exit.*
[*Music Cue #10C*])

OPAL. (*Suddenly alarmed.*) A baby?! ... to Elsie Fairchild?! ... Oh, no!! I have so much work to do! (*SHE climbs down quickly, and dashes away.*)

NARRATORS. (*To audience.*)
A new baby had come to *Elsie* and not the thought-girl.
Maybe the angels had had a mix-up.
This was a big "cal-lamb-of-tea!"
Now, there was only one thing to do!

(*A BABY cries. A WOMAN shouts. OPAL dashes through, clutching a baby in her arms. SHE is pursued by the young HUSBAND OF ELSIE. HE is wearing long johns, trying to pull up his pants as HE chases after OPAL—tripping and falling en route. Ad-lib commotion as the scene changes.)*

HUSBAND OF ELSIE. Stop! Stop! Come back here with our baby! (*HE chases her to:*)

Sadie McKibben's Shanty

(SADIE is scrubbing clothes. The GOSSIP SISTERS are there, bringing more laundry.
OPAL bursts in with the baby. Laundry flies. More ad-lib commotion.
Simultaneously:)

OPAL.	SADIE.	GOSSIP SISTERS.	HUSBAND.
(*Running to SADIE for protection.*) Sadie McKibben! Sadie McKibben!	Mercy, what have ye!? (*Etc.*)	(*Gasp.*) Oh, land sakes alive! (*Etc.*)	Stop, I tell you! Come back here with our baby! You little good-fer-nuthin'! (*Etc.*)

(The furor breaks off suddenly, when ELSIE'S HUSBAND barges in.)

HUSBAND OF ELSIE. ... Damn you, girl!!!

(GOSSIP SISTERS, with hands over their ears, gasp.)

HUSBAND OF ELSIE. (*Trying to hold his pants up.*) Oh, uh .... pardon me, Ladies. But, that little foreign girl stole our baby from its cradle while it was nappin'!

(Reaction.)

OPAL. (*Indignantly.*) No I didn't. This isn't your baby. (*To ELSIE'S HUSBAND.*) Your wife had someone *else's* baby!

(*General reaction. Simultaneously:*)

GOSSIP SISTERS. **HUSBAND.**
(*Gasp.*) Gutter talk! Why, you lil' tramp!
Gutter talk! (*Ad-libs. Etc.*) (*Ad-libs. Etc.*)

SADIE. (*Forcefully silencing the uproar.*) All of ye, stop!! (*To OPAL.*) Now, Opal. Give back the babe.

OPAL. I won't! The angels meant this baby for the thought-girl!

SADIE. The thought-girl?

OPAL. Miss Ryden.

SADIE. I see.

GOSSIP SISTERS. Well, *we* don't.

OPAL. Neither did Elsie. She looked confusion when I told her the baby wasn't hers.

SADIE. Opal ... Miss Ryden can't have a babe until she has a husband.

OPAL. A *husband?* How does a *husband* make a baby come?

GOSSIP SISTERS. If they have to ask the question, they're too young to know the answer!

(*Ad-lib furor. Simultaneously:*)

GOSSIP SISTERS. **HUSBAND.**
Wash her mouth out! Why you little gutter
(*Ad-libs. Etc.*) snipe! (*Ad-libs. Etc.*)

(*In the uproar, the GOSSIP SISTERS take the husband's hands to offer comfort, making his pants drop. The GOSSIP SISTERS swoon. More commotion.*)

SADIE. Silence! Ye'll not say another word again' the child! (*To OPAL.*) Opal, it is time ye start to learn there is order in things. And that means babies are always brought to the right folks.

OPAL. Then, this is not the thought-girl's baby?

(Simultaneously:)

	GOSSIP	
SADIE.	**SISTERS.**	**HUSBAND.**
No.	I should say not!	Hell, no!

OPAL. (*Thinks, then hands the baby back to ELSIE'S HUSBAND.*) Elsie will be glad to know she can keep it.

(Simultaneously:)

	GOSSIP	
SADIE.	**SISTERS.**	**HUSBAND.**
Aye.	I never!	(*Grabbing the baby.*) Stupid girl!

(ELSIE'S HUSBAND stomps out.)

OPAL. (*To SADIE.*) But, when will the angels bring the *thought-girl* a baby?

SADIE. When it is time.

OPAL. Maybe the man that wears gray neckties should ask the tree fairies to bring her one.

GOSSIP SISTERS. The man that wears gray neckties?

SADIE. That's Andrew Givens.

OPAL. The tree fairies bring him many bunches of *fleurs*.

SADIE. (*Again, to the GOSSIP SISTERS.*) That's flowers.

GOSSIP SISTERS. Oh, everybody in town knows about those flowers. Folks say he picks them for Laura Ryden.

SADIE. The mill-owner's daughter?

OPAL. The thought-girl?

GOSSIP SISTERS. The same. (*Confidentially.*) It's (*Whisper.*) L.O.V.E. (*Normal voice.*) But, both of 'em shy as colts. Such a (*Each takes a different word; simultaneously.*) shame/pity. (*Reaction. Reversing their words.*) Pity/shame. (*Quick shrug. [Music Cue #10D] THEY exit.*)

OPAL. (*Suddenly eager to leave.*) There are hurries in my feet. I must go now.

SADIE. I understand. But, mind yir ways, child.

OPAL. (*Hurries outside. Taking her mouse from her pocket.*) Did you hear that, Felix Mendelssohn?! It's (*Whispers.*) L.O.V.E.! (*Normal voice.*) I only hope the thought-girl can spell.

(*OPAL dashes off and SADIE exits as NECKTIES and two MALE NARRATORS enter. Dissolve to:*)

The General Store

(*NECKTIES enters the General Store. The BELL dings.*)

NECKTIES. Did it come today?

GENERAL STORE OWNER. (*Handing NECK-TIES a small package; slaps NECKTIES on the back and chortles.*) Yup. It came. Direct from Sears and Roebuck!

NECKTIES. Thanks. (*HE takes the package, and opens it slowly. It is so wonderful, HE is nearly overwhelmed. LIGHTS focus in on him as HE sings.*)

The Mill Town, the Forest Path, the Barber Shop, and the House of the Thought-Girl

*(The following song is about the intersection of two plot
    lines: NECKTIES mustering up the courage and the
    words to propose while OPAL independently plays
    match-maker and brings him the THOUGHT-GIRL.
Perhaps one of the NARRATORS accompanies on
    guitar.)*

[Music Cue #11: EVERYBODY'S LOOKING
FOR LOVE]

NECKTIES. *(Out front; as if to the Thought-Girl;
practicing his proposal.)*
I HEARD ME A CRICKET
AS HE STIRRED IN THE THICKET,
MAKING MUSIC ALL ALONE.

I HEARD ME THE WHISTLE
OF A BIRD IN THE THISTLE,
FOR A BIRD TO CALL HIS OWN.

AND WHEN THAT BIRD
GAVE OUT HIS CALL,
AND LAID A CLAIM FOR A MATE, HE DID
THE SAME AS THE KATYDID—
AND I CLAIM, DON'T WE ALL?

*(NECKTIES moves to one side, where HE continues to
    sing. Meanwhile, as if in split-screen, we focus on
    OPAL running breathlessly up to the house of the
    THOUGHT-GIRL, where the THOUGHT-GIRL is in
    the midst of cooking.*
OPAL mimes pounding on the door, while a
    NARRATOR provides the sound effects. The
    THOUGHT-GIRL answers. OPAL mimes telling her
    about the flowers, but the THOUGHT-GIRL doesn't
    understand.)*

NECKTIES. (*To audience.*)
EVERYBODY'S LOOKING FOR LOVE,
I SAY THEY'RE LOOKING,
LOOKING HIGH AND LOOKING LOW.

EVERYBODY'S LOOKING FOR LOVE,
I SAY THEY'RE LOOKING,
LOOKING EVERYWHERE THEY GO.

EVERYBODY'S LOOKING FOR LOVE,
I SAY THEY'RE LOOKING,
BUT IT'S ONLY FAIR THEY KNOW:

NO USE LOOKING 'ROUND ON YOUR OWN,
'CAUSE NO ONE EVER FOUND IT ALONE.
IF EVERYBODY ONLY KNEW,
THEY'D GO LOOKING TWO BY TWO,
WHENEVER THEY GO LOOKING FOR LOVE.

(*Finally, in exasperation, OPAL grasps the THOUGHT-GIRL by the hand and whisks her away. THEY exit. We focus back on NECKTIES. As HE sings, HE gathers bunches of wildflowers and leaves them along the path near the Thought-Girl's home.*)

NECKTIES.
I SPIED ME A RAVEN
AND HIS BRIDE IN THEIR HAVEN
MADE OF TWIGS, ABOVE THE KNOLL.

I SPIED ME A FROG UP—
ON THE SIDE OF A BOG, A-
BOUT TO DIVE INTO HIS HOLE.

AND, THOUGH THAT HOLE
WAS MUD AND LOAM,
THAT FROG WAS CLEVERLY CROAKING,
"BE IT EVER SO SOAKING,

THERE JUST AIN'T NO LOAM LIKE HOME."

*(Now we focus on OPAL leading the THOUGHT-GIRL
along the walking path, finding the bunches of flowers
NECKTIES left. THEY do not see him and HE does
not see them.*
*Meanwhile NECKTIES is besieged by the GOSSIP
SISTERS, the GENERAL STORE OWNER, and the
MILL TOWN BARBER, who fuss over his
appearance. The BARBER sits him down on a stump,
and gives him a shave, while the GOSSIP SISTERS
inspect behind his ears, check his fingernails, slick
back his hair, etc., until he meets with their
enthusiastic approval.)*

NECKTIES and NARRATORS. *(Plus available
offstage voices.)*
EVERYBODY'S LOOKING FOR LOVE,
I SAY THEY'RE LOOKING,
LOOKING HIGH AND LOOKING LOW.

EVERYBODY'S LOOKING FOR LOVE,
I SAY THEY'RE LOOKING,
LOOKING EVERYWHERE THEY GO.

EVERYBODY'S LOOKING FOR LOVE,
I SAY THEY'RE LOOKING,
BUT IT'S ONLY FAIR THEY KNOW:

NO USE LOOKING 'ROUND ON YOUR OWN,
'CAUSE NO ONE EVER FOUND IT ALONE.
IF EVERYBODY ONLY KNEW,
THEY'D GO LOOKING TWO BY TWO,
WHENEVER THEY GO LOOKING FOR LOVE.

*(OPAL and the THOUGHT-GIRL exit with the bunches
of flowers.*

We focus back on NECKTIES, who goes to crouch
beside a creek—perhaps represented by the edge of the
stage.)

NECKTIES.
I HEARD ME THE SWISHES
OF THE TURTLES AND FISHES,
THAT WERE DANCING IN THE BROOK.

WHERE THE WATER WAS RISING,
WHAT I SAW WAS SURPRISING,
WHEN I WENT TO TAKE A LOOK.

(HE and the OTHERS lean forward to take a look in the
creek.)

NECKTIES.
I SAW A FACE
COME INTO VIEW.

AND THAT FACE SHOWN FULL OF TROUBLES.
YUP, IT SURE WAS A CASE. IT
WAS ALONE WITH THE BUBBLES.
I SAID,

(To the reflection.)

NECKTIES.
"SIR, BETTER FACE IT,
LIFE IS ONLY FOR DOUBLES
FIND A MERMAID TO CHASE.
    ALL.
IT'S WHAT I'D DO,
IF I WERE YOU!

(NECKTIES shows the town folk the ring. The MEN
congratulate NECKTIES and boost his courage. The
MILL TOWN FOLKS put the finishing touches on

*Neckties' appearance—dusting him off; straightening
his tie, spit-polishing his boots, etc.
Meanwhile, we see OPAL leading the THOUGHT-GIRL
closer and closer through the forest to the clearing.)*

NECKTIES and NARRATORS.
EVERYBODY'S LOOKING FOR LOVE,
I SAY THEY'RE LOOKING,
LOOKING HIGH AND LOOKING LOW.

EVERYBODY'S LOOKING FOR LOVE,
I SAY THEY'RE LOOKING,
LOOKING EVERYWHERE THEY GO.

*(NECKTIES and the THOUGHT-GIRL see each other.
THEY are nervous and hesitant, but their FRIENDS
prod them together.)*

EVERYBODY'S LOOKING FOR LOVE,
I SAY THEY'RE LOOKING,
BUT IT'S ONLY FAIR THEY KNOW:

NO USE LOOKING 'ROUND ON YOUR OWN,
'CAUSE NO ONE EVER FOUND IT ALONE.
IF EVERYBODY ONLY KNEW,
THEY'D GO LOOKING TWO BY TWO,
WHENEVER THEY GO LOOKING FOR LOVE.
FOR LOVE ...

*(OPAL gives the THOUGHT-GIRL a gentle push
towards NECKTIES, then joins the MILL TOWN
FOLKS.
NECKTIES kneels and takes out the ring as the MILL
TOWN FOLKS look on.)*

NARRATORS and OPAL.
EVERYBODY'S LOOKING FOR LOVE,
I SAY THEY'RE LOOKING,

LOOKING HIGH AND LOOKING LOW.

EVERYBODY'S LOOKING FOR LOVE,
I SAY THEY'RE LOOKING,
LOOKING EVERYWHERE THEY GO

EVERYBODY'S LOOKING FOR LOVE,
I SAY THEY'RE LOOKING,
BUT IT'S ONLY FAIR THEY KNOW:

NO USE LOOKING 'ROUND ON YOUR OWN,
'CAUSE NO ONE EVER FOUND IT ALONE.
IF EVERYBODY ONLY KNEW,
THEY'D GO LOOKING TWO BY TWO,
WHENEVER THEY GO LOOKING FOR LOVE.
   NECKTIES. (*Sung in counterpoint to the chorus.*)
THAT SEARS AND ROEBUCK WEDDING BAND
ON PAGE ONE HUNDRED THREE.
GOLD ELECTRO-PLATED,
WITH A LIFETIME GUARANTEE.

A FELLA NEEDS A DREAM TO DREAM,
ESPECIALLY IF HE'S POOR.
THAT'S THE THING
THAT CATALOGUES
AND VERY PRETTY GIRLS ARE FOR.

(*NECKTIES puts the ring on the THOUGHT-GIRL's
   finger. The GOSSIP SISTERS wax romantic and dab
   away a tear of joy.*)

   ALL.
IF EVERYBODY ONLY KNEW,
THEY'D GO LOOKING TWO BY TWO,
WHENEVER THEY GO LOOKING FOR
LOVE!

[Music Cue #11A]

*(The BLIND GIRL enters as the MILL TOWN FOLKS
    disperse. SHE senses that something has taken place.
Lost in each other, NECKTIES and the THOUGHT-
    GIRL kiss. As THEY start to stroll off hand in hand,
    the THOUGHT-GIRL turns and throws OPAL one of
    the bouquets. OPAL catches it and giggles.)*

GIRL THAT HAS NO SEEING. Opal? What
happened?

OPAL. The man that wears gray neckties has got his
wife.

GIRL THAT HAS NO SEEING. What do you
mean?

OPAL. He gave the thought-girl a ring of gold, and
she is going to be his wife.

THE GIRL THAT HAS NO SEEING. The
thought-girl?

OPAL. Laura Ryden.

GIRL THAT HAS NO SEEING. Laura Ryden?

OPAL. Yes ... There are trouble lines on your face ...
What is wrong?

GIRL THAT HAS NO SEEING. Nothing.

OPAL. I have thinks you are going to have cry-feels.

GIRL THAT HAS NO SEEING. Nonsense ...
Why would I cry?

OPAL. (*Shrugging.*) I have not imagines.

GIRL THAT HAS NO SEEING. And I have too
many "imagines," Opal. That's the problem. When you
can't see ... all you can do is imagine.

OPAL. I don't understand.

GIRL THAT HAS NO SEEING. Go on, Opal,
please. (*OPAL doesn't go.*) Please. I just want to be
alone.

OPAL. Did I say something bad?

GIRL THAT HAS NO SEEING. It has nothing
to do with you. It has nothing to do with anybody. Just,
please, go. I don't feel like playing anymore.

(SELENA rushes away in tears into the forest. OPAL leaves hesitantly, somewhat mystified.
SELENA wanders through the trees, feeling her way with her cane. The MUSIC turns eerily foreboding as SHE enacts the following narration:)

THE DEEP FOREST

NARRATORS. *(To audience.)*
The blind girl walked deeper and deeper into the forest alone,
going farther and farther into the deserted timber.
VOICE OF SELENA'S MOTHER. *(Calling; as if from a great distance.)* Seleeeenaaa!
NARRATORS.
Leaving the path, she wandered aimlessly,
hour after hour.

(The LIGHTING grows dark and ominous. It is DUSK. The tree branches cast long, strange shadows on the forest floor.)

SELENA'S MOTHER. Seleeeenaaaa! Where are you?! Seleeeeenaaa?!

(SELENA kneels down and takes a candle from her pocket—the candle OPAL gave her. SHE lights it.)

NARRATORS.
The blind girl lit a small candle of hope,
as Opal had done.
And in the dead heat of summer,
in search of hope,
the blind girl lost her way.

(SELENA carries the candle as feels her way with the cane. SHE becomes disoriented. Lost. SHE panics.

Then trips. SHE drops the candle. The ground catches FIRE.)

THE GIRL THAT HAS NO SEEING. No!

(The forest fire spreads—represented by the NARRATORS, who surround SELENA, closing in on her little by little as the sound of crackling FLAMES grows ever louder.)

NARRATORS.
A small flame ignited. Selena sensed danger.
Which way was safety?
Was it this way?
Or this?

(SELENA tries to escape the NARRATORS, but THEY pursue her—their hands reaching out to her like flames. THEY corner, surround, and, eventually, trap her.)

NARRATORS.
The fire spread.
(All.)
Smoke ... Crackling flames ... Selena tried to escape.
THE GIRL THAT HAS NO SEEING. Help, somebody! Help! Mother! (*Etc. Ad-lib.*)
VOICE OF SELENA'S MOTHER. Seleeenaa!? Where are you?!

(Soon, SELENA is engulfed in flames. SHE lets out a hideous scream and whirls away—disappearing into the smoke and flames.
We hear SHOUTING and COMMOTION as the THOUGHT-GIRL, SADIE, and the MAMMA enter, joined by the LUMBER CAMP FOLKS. THEY stagger through the heat and smoke, braving the burning forest as THEY try to beat out the fire with

rugs and burlap sacks. In the flickering firelight, we can't distinguish characters—only chaos. COUGHING. SCREAMING. FALLING TREES. Danger.)

ALL. (*Ad-lib furor; such as:.*) Get more water! We need blankets, rugs, anything! It's spreading to the mill town! Somebody go warn 'em! (*As a tree falls.*) Look out!! More buckets! This smoke! I can't breathe! (*Etc.*)

ONE OF THE LUMBER CAMP FOLKS. There's a girl in there!

THE MAMMA. What?

ONE OF THE LUMBER CAMP FOLKS. There's a girl in the fire!

THE MAMMA. (*Runs off shouting.*) Opal! Opal! (*Ad-lib.*)

(As the MAMMA exits, NECKTIES runs in commanding a party of MEN.)

NECKTIES. Take those buckets and douse the clearing. The rest a you, break up an' warn the folks along the ridge.

OPAL. (*Enters and runs in past NECKTIES. Calling.*) Girl that has no seeing!

NECKTIES. (*Grabs OPAL roughly.*) Hey, where you goin'?!

OPAL. To save the girl that has no seeing! Her mother said she is lost in the forest!

NECKTIES. Go home, girl!

OPAL. Please, let me go!

NECKTIES. I said, go home!

OPAL. She needs me!

NECKTIES. (*Interrupting*) Opal, I said ta—(*Pause.*) ... the blind girl is gone.

OPAL. Gone?

NECKTIES. She got caught in the brush fire.

OPAL. No.

NECKTIES. We found her lyin' in the hollow. It was too late.

OPAL. Too late?

NECKTIES. She's dead, Opal, an' that's that. I'm sorry. (*Sternly.*) Now, go home. (*To the others.*) Come on, men, let's go!

(*THEY run out, leaving OPAL alone in shock.*
SADIE appears at another part of the stage. SHE is weary and disheveled—her face smeared with ashes; her dress torn.)

SADIE. (*Going to OPAL.*) Opal.

OPAL. (*Feebly; in disbelief; still in shock.*) No. No.

SADIE. (*Shaking OPAL.*) Wake, child, wake.

OPAL. It cannot be. *I* did teach her to walk in the forest ... *I* made her go *away*

[Music Cue #12: WHY DO I SEE GOD?]

SADIE. Yir ne're to blame yirself. Yir a child. She was not.

OPAL. I only tried to make earth glad, and I made her go away. (*Bursting into tears.*) Now she is gone, like Mother and Father.

SADIE. Aye.

OPAL. She is gone, like Peter Paul Rubens.

SADIE. Aye.

OPAL. And they are never coming back! Never! Just like the mamma said all along!

SADIE. Aye.

OPAL. You said to search for a sign! I believed you! Why can't I see it? Why? Why?

SADIE. (*Searching for the words.*)
WHY DO I SEE GOD,
IN A GODLESS WORLD?
WHY DO I SEE GOOD,

WHEN GRIEVING EYES WITH TEARS ARE
  PEARLED?

(SADIE reaches for OPAL. OPAL pulls away.)

OH, MY LITTLE CHILD,
GOOD IS SEEN IN GOOD'S RETURN,
FOR THE WORLD IS MADE OF CYCLES,
AS YE NOW MUST LEARN.

(OPAL turns away. SHE doesn't want to hear.)

    SADIE. *(Sitting wearily.)*
AND YEAR BY YEAR WE REAP, WE TOIL,
WITH FURROWED BROW ON FURROWED SOIL—
OUR BACKS ALL BENT,
LIKE SICKLE BLADES AGAINST THE SKY—

AND YEAR BY YEAR, AS YEARS GO BY,
WE WORK OUR FIELDS, AND WONDER, "WHY?!"
BUT ANSWERS LIE IN EVERY FIELD,
WHERE EVERY STEM IS POINTING SKYWARD.

*(SADIE rises, moving slowly away from OPAL to
  observe the devastation, lost in a prophetic vision.)*

    SADIE. *(With passion and anger.)*
WHY WILL I SEE LIFE
'TIL MY DYING BREATH?
WHY WILL I SEE LIFE,
WHEN ALL OF LIFE IS FILLED WITH DEATH?

OH, MY LITTLE CHILD,
EARTH IS HEAVEN'S LEARNING PLACE,
WHERE ETERNITY IS TAUGHT
BY HEAVEN'S ROD.

(OPAL looks at SADIE.)

FOR MY CHILD, MY CHILD,
THOUGH DEATH'S OWN PEN
MAY LINE MY FACE,
WHEN I LOOK UPON A CHILD,
I SEE THE FACE OF GOD.

*(Distant smoke and burning embers. SADIE holds out her
arms. OPAL considers a moment, then comes to her
slowly. THEY embrace.*
*Just as the song is about to end, the MAMMA rushes in,
calling desperately.)*

THE MAMMA. Opal! Opal! Where are you?! Opal!?
*(She sees OPAL. Runs, falls to her knees and embraces
her. In tears.)* They said a girl was killed in the fire ...
And I was so afraid ... I thought, fer a minute—

*(Suddenly, OPAL pushes away from the MAMMA and
backs up towards SADIE. The MAMMA is startled.)*

THE MAMMA. Why didn't chu answer me when I
called you, Opal?!
OPAL. That is not my name. *(SHE looks to SADIE.)*
My name is Françoise.

*(Long silence. The MAMMA registers bitter displeasure
then glares accusingly at SADIE. The MAMMA rises
to her feet. Grabs OPAL by the hand.)*

THE MAMMA. *(Muttered harshly.)* Come on.

*(SHE tugs OPAL away, as the NARRATORS enter and
the LIGHTS change. The scene dissolves to:)*

SEQUENCE SEVEN — Days Later

Mrs. Potter's Shanty and The Lumber Camp

([Music Cue #12A]
The NARRATORS, as the lumber camp folks, begin
tearing down camp and leaving town. THEY pass by
in a procession, carrying their trunks and belongings.
MUSIC underscores throughout.)

NARRATORS. (*To audience.*)
The lumber camp ... Days later.
The forest had been destroyed.
The mill town folks began tearing down camp ... and
moving on.

(OPAL steps forward.)

NARRATORS.
And, on the final page of her diary, Opal wrote:
OPAL. (*Out front; sadness still lingering.*) Dear Angel
Mother and Father ... The forest that was, ... is *gone.*

(Passing by together, NECKTIES and the THOUGHT-
GIRL step out of the procession and come to OPAL.)

NECKTIES. The whole reason Laurie and me heard
weddin' bells was thanks ta you, Opal. Ya said ya was
gonna git me a wife, an' you did.
THOUGHT-GIRL. And I have a special secret ...
It's something the angels let me know ahead of time ...
by this time next year, they're going to bring me a *baby.*
OPAL. (*Quietly; rousing only a little.*) That gives me
joy-feels.
NECKTIES. Be good, little girl.

(HE pats her on the head. NECKTIES and the
THOUGHT-GIRL rejoin the procession.

SADIE MCKIBBEN steps out of the procession, carrying her washboard and a bundle of possessions, and comes to OPAL.)

SADIE. The stars only know where Sadie may go.

OPAL. Take me with you, Sadie McKibben.

SADIE. Child, I'm poor and old. If I should take ye, ye would all too soon be penniless and alone.

OPAL. You're not old, Sadie McKibben. The freckles on your wrinkled face are as lovely as the stars in the Milky Way ... Take me with you.

(The MAMMA enters, laden with satchels and bundles. SHE stops when she hears this last phrase, unseen by OPAL and SADIE.)

SADIE. I should tell ye no, but I haven't the strength. Though I've not the means, I've a mind to take ye. Ye can come with me or no. Ye decide. Ye decide what be in the stars.

THE MAMMA. (*Comes to OPAL and SADIE. Pretending she didn't hear; strict.*) It's movin' day. Don't dally, girl. (*To SADIE.*) We're movin' ta Lonesome Pine Lumber camp, ta live with my brother. (*To OPAL.*) Only, don't chu give him no sass, 'cause he don't love children like I do. Now, none but yer necessary things can go. That's yer McGuffie's Reader, yer apron, yer calico dress, an' yer shoes. (*Rummaging impatiently through a satchel.*) Oh, an' while I was packin', I found this. (*SHE pulls out Opal's diary.*)

(OPAL gives a small gasp. Looks to SADIE for help.)

THE MAMMA. What is it?

OPAL. My diary.

THE MAMMA. Uh huh.

OPAL. I write in it.

THE MAMMA. Uh huh.

OPAL. (*Looks to SADIE; then to the MAMMA.*) It's a necessary thing.

THE MAMMA. Uh huh. (*SHE pages through the diary accusingly.*) I see ya been writin' somethin' 'bout me. 'Spose ya tell me what's so necessary 'bout this, huh?! (*SHE shoves the diary into Opal's hands.*) Read it.

OPAL. (*Reading.*) "There is no song in the mamma's heart. Somebody took it away. I'm saving my pennies to buy her a singing lesson."

THE MAMMA. (*Thinks. Decides. Puts the diary in her satchel.*) Well, why not? Maybe it'll keep ya outa trouble. (*SHE throws a look at SADIE. Then to OPAL:*) I'll wait fer ya by the road. (*The MAMMA goes to one side of the playing area to wait.*)

OPAL. (*To SADIE.*) Is Felix Mendelssohn a necessary thing?

SADIE. Ye decide, child, where it is best he go.

OPAL. And where is it best I go? With the mamma? Or with you ?

SADIE. Ye decide—what shall make earth the most glad. I'll be waiting fir ye in the clearing.

(As OPAL takes her mouse from her pocket, SADIE goes far upstage—to wait.)

OPAL. (*To the Mouse.*) Maybe it is best I leave you in the forest with the other mice. They need you. But, don't be sad, Felix Mendelssohn. I shall always be with you *inside*.

NARRATORS. (*Narrating the action; to audience.*) Opal returned to the forest cathedral one last time.

(The scene around OPAL transforms into:)

The Charred Remains of the Forest Cathedral

*(Eerie, DEATH-MUSIC. Burned tree trunks. The
LIGHTING dims. Long, stark shadows of bone-like
branches.*
*OPAL walks slowly through the scorched rubble aghast
at the desolation; sad and frightened.)*

NARRATORS.
The forest was black and desolate.
The ground was charred.
The trees were scorched and skeletal.
She heard their death song echoing through the
canyons.

*(OPAL arrives at the place where Michael Angelo once
stood. He is gone—leaving cinders and blackened
debris.)*

NARRATORS.
She saw that Michael Angelo, whose arms were once
so strong,
was now blackened, brittle, and bone-like,
the empty color of shadows.

*(As OPAL kneels down and releases her mouse,
something on the ground catches her eye.)*

NARRATORS.
But, as she knelt down to release Felix Mendelssohn,
she discovered something wonderful.

*(OPAL sees a little, white lily growing up through the
ashes. Perhaps one of the NARRATORS simply
kneels down and reaches out to the ground before
OPAL, holding the lily upright under a PINSPOT
light.)*

NARRATORS.
There, among the blackened debris,
was a *small, white, lily.*
It had survived the forest fire ...
and bloomed that day.
OPAL. (*Kneels slowly before the lily—starring at it
in wonder. After a pause; whispering in awe.*) Peter Paul
Rubens ... (*Slowly.*) I have found ... your ... soul.

(*SADIE and the MAMMA are still waiting. THEY watch
      OPAL from a distance—standing in separate pools of
      LIGHT.*
We hear the MUSIC BOX repeating its tune.
*OPAL gently digs up the lily and cups it in her hands.
      She rises slowly and turns upstage, facing the
      MAMMA and SADIE.*
*As if choosing, OPAL first looks towards SADIE. Then
      SHE looks towards the MAMMA. Pause. OPAL
      considers.*
*Then, deciding, OPAL runs to SADIE. The MAMMA
      turns away and sits dejectedly.*
*OPAL gives SADIE the lily. SADIE recognizes it as the
      sign. THEY embrace. SADIE leaves.*
*Then OPAL walks slowly, cautiously to the MAMMA.
      SHE picks up one of the mamma's bundles. The
      MAMMA turns and sees her. Registers. Then calmly
      rises to leave.*)

THE MAMMA. Let's go ... (*Pause.*) Francine.

(*THEY leave. LIGHTS fade.*)

THE END

COSTUME PLOT

Note: This list is what we did in the New York production, but is not the only creative solution to the show. The period is 1904, but this lumber town in Oregon would be several years behind in silhouette. For the most part, the people made their own clothes, which can be simple or quite detailed.

OPAL/FRANÇOISE
White crepe eyelet 1904 little girl's dress with antique laces and insertions, puff sleeves, standing collar with lace edge. Pink silk belt. Easy to remove onstage. Dyed to look wet and distressed from shipwreck. Pink hair bow. Brown lace-up boots. Off-white cotton slip.

1st change done onstage by Mamma:
> Man's long john top (faded pink), hair tied in braids (over slip)

2nd change done onstage by Mamma for school:
> Add flour sack "pinafore" with drawstring casing at neck, and flour labels on front and back over long john top and slip.

3rd change done onstage by Mamma for Social:
> Add patchwork quilt pinafore with feed bag label pockets to above. Add blue calico bonnet with ties.

Additional dark red knit cap for winter.

BLIND GIRL/SELENA
Grey-blue tweed jumper type dress with black scallop trim and matching fabric belt. Mattress ticking shirtwaist with standing collar. Black large hair bow. Pink bloomers and black tights. For Social: change to white blouse. For winter: black shawl. Note: We used wire rimmed dark glasses with black screenwire instead of glass. Gray rough linen work apron with pocket. Black lace-up boots. Hair parted in center and back in curls.

SADIE McKIBBEN
Brown and black diamond check sleeveless bustle jacket (1880's) distressed. Earthtones patchwork pattern full skirt. Gray-green raw silk blouse. Gray tights. Black laced boots. Teal shawl for winter. Large brown velvet hat with brown bow trim for leaving. Red petticoat with lace trim. Red bloomers. Hair should be gray or white, as old as actress can look.

MAMMA/MRS. POTTER
Dark red robe with tie. Long john top and gray-green petticoat under robe. Flat lace-up mens shoes with mens socks.

1st change: Gray raw silk blouse with color print patches in lining. Same petticoat skirt. Dark green apron swag tucked into belt. Faded stripe apron with pocket and ties.

2nd change (Social): Dark red dress with full sleeves and matching belt. Add dark red cardigan sweater.

Add brown silk 1890's jacket to above for leaving.
Butcher's apron with dyed "blood stains" for slaughter.
Pale orange rough shawl for "winter."
Green cut-off gloves. Green short cape.

THOUGHT GIRL/MISS RYDEN
Off-white cotton eyelet blouse with ribbon tie. Dark blue wool skirt with gray lace trim. Black shaped belt. Beige with navy plain bibbed apron with ties.

1st change: Blue and pink floral on beige background calico dress with dotted net on pale blue neck insert. Brown suede belt, for social. White petticoat, white bloomers, tan and brown laced boots.

2nd change: Same blue skirt with lavender blouse.

Add dark gray with red stripe jacket for leaving.

As "Angel Mother": off-white dotted net 1900's gown with antique lace trim, dotted with aurora beads. Gray satin belt with flower trim. Cameo pin at neck. Costume has petticoat built in and is made for quick change. Large horsehair hat with off-white, pale orange, pale green flowers, leaves and net veiling covers face. Off-white gloves. Same boots and tan hose.

NARRATOR/GOSSIP SISTER /SCHOOLTEACHER

Base costume consisting of calico cotton 1890's blouse. Teal stripe full skirt, black shaped belt, gray tights.

Add to this: brown tweed wool jacket, tan poke bonnet for narrator and leaving.

For Gossip Sister: reversible iridescent teal cape/apron, when reversed can be snapped to waist belt to become an apron. Bi-focal glasses in trick pocket.

For Schoolteacher: long mauve print skirt which starts as empire apron or "smock" and is pulled down to waist to form long skirt standing on a barrel. Black shawl.

For Social: add natural straw hat.

For winter: add plum shawl.

NARRATOR/GOSSIP SISTER /SCHOOLGIRL

Base costume consisting of calico cotton print blouse, maroon plaid full skirt. Brown waist belt, gray tights, black laced boots.

Add to this: tan tweed wool jacket, straw bonnet with brown and lavender trim for narrator and leaving.

For Gossip Sister: iridescent gold cape/apron, when reversed can be snapped to waist belt to become apron. Bi-focal glasses in pocket.

For schoolgirl: print cotton apron becomes pinafore with hidden eyelet ruffle straps. Add clip-on piece of hair curls with red bow.

For Social: add natural straw hat.

For winter: add brown shawl.

NECKTIES/ANDREW GIVENS
Faded red and blue plaid full-sleeve shirt, period blue jeans with wide suspenders, long underwear, gray four-in-hand necktie.

For Social: add brown leather vest and white shirt.

For Marriage Proposal: add blue sack coat, gray western tie.

For Winter: add plaid wool scarf.

As "Angel Father": gray cutaway suit, stripe ascot tie, pale gray Homburg hat, walking stick, gray gloves. This is fixed for quick change.

Brown high work boots.

NARRATOR/GENERAL STOREKEEPER /HUSBAND
Base costume of pale orange rough full sleeve shirt, olive rough pants with wide suspenders, long john underwear, rough period vest, high boots, 1860's black derby.

For General Store Man: add green visor, apron, sleeveguards.

For School Child: large Eaton collar with blue bow on clip

For Winter: wool scarf and wool gloves.

For Social: change of lighter color shirt and string tie.

For leaving: rough tweed jacket and derby.

NARRATOR/MAN/SQUARE DANCE CALLER
Base costume of brown raw silk rough shirt with full sleeves, burnt orange stripe rough pants, long underwear top under wide leather belt, brown rough high boots.

For Man in Shanty: gray rough poncho with large brimmed hat made to look wet.

For School child: large Eaton collar with large blue bow on neck clip.

For Winter: maroon wool scarf.

For Square Dance Caller: Change to off-white full sleeve shirt and dark blue string tie.

For Barber: shirt sleeve garters and barber's apron.

For leaving: rough distressed jacket and olive worn fedora.

PROPERTY PLOT

Prologue:
Square lanterns (2) (Narrators)
Music box (Angel Father)
Walking stick (Angel Father)
Parasol (Angel Mother)
Crate (to sit on) (Narrator)
Hand-held fresnel (ship's searchlight) (Narrator)

Sequence One:
Whiskey flask (Man)
Hat (Man)
Shotgun (Narrator)
Blanket (The Mama)
Roll of butcher's paper (Narrator)
Wax pencils (3 crayons)
Walking stick (Angel Father)
Parasol (Angel Mother)
Crash box (sound effect of the pig breaking out of his pen) (Percussionist)

Sequence Two:
(Assorted tools and implements of logging and domestic labor such as:)
Two-handled bow saw (Lumberjack & Neckties)
Axe (Lumberjack)
Tea towel (Selena)
Rag (to scrub floor) (Lumber camp woman)
Shovel (Lumber camp woman)
Broom (Thought-Girl)
Bowl (for snapping green beans—the beans are mimed) (Selena)
Bowl and spoon (for "mush") (The Mama)
Burlap feedbag (to slop the hog—the feed is mimed) (The Mama)
Rug beater (Narrator)
Scrub brush (The Mama)

Bucket (The Mama)

Can of Bon Ami (The Mama)

Egg basket (without eggs—the eggs are mimed) (The Mama)

Bells (2) (tiny bells to ring when the "door" to the General Store is opened)(Narrator)

Sears and Roebuck catalogue (General Store Owner)

Bunches of wildflowers (2) (Neckties and Thought-girl)

Washtub and scrubbing board (Narrator)

Stool (Narrator)

Laundry (to scrub) (Sadie)

Crates (to sit or stand on) (Narrators)

Sequence Three:

Pointer (Narrator as Teacher)

(The following items are used for the school children to sit on:)

Crates (2) (Narrator, School Children)

Small stool (Narrator, School Children)

Washtub (overturned and used for Opal to sit on)

Washtub and scrubbing board (the water is mimed) (Narrator)

Laundry lines hung with wash (Narrators)

Small stool (Narrator)

Petticoat and rag (to scrub in the washtub and to scrub the pig) (Sadie)

Clothes pins (Sadie)

Assorted laundry (to hold) (Gossip Sisters)

Diary (brown paper bound with string) (Narrator)

Crayon (Opal)

Watering can (Narrator)

Sequence Four:

Baby bundled in a blanket (Thought-girl)

Round lanterns (2) (Narrators)

Branch (becomes Selena's walking stick) (Narrator)

Kindling (to snap when Opal "breaks off" the branch) Narrator

Matches (Opal)
Candle (Opal)
Butcher's knife (The Mama)

Sequence Five:
Assorted winter scarves, hats and gloves (Cast)
(assorted tools, implements of logging and domestic labor, such as:)
Butcher churn (The Mama)
Broom (Sadie)
Axe (Narrator as lumberjack)
Pocket knife and whitling stick (Narrator as lumberjack)
Large barrel (Narrators "warm" their hands over it)

Sequence Six:
Bunch of wildflowers (small bouquet of early spring flowers) (Neckties)

Sequence Seven:
Locket pendant on necklace chain (The Mama)
Meat grinder (than can be assembled) (The Mama)
Bowl (for the meat—which is mimed) (The Mama)
Crate (to hold the grinder and bowl. Later it is stood on end and the bowl placed on it.) (The Mama)
Barrel (on which the meat grinder is set) (Narrator)
Baby wrapped in blanket (Opal)
Laundry lines hung with wash (Narrators)
Assorted laundry (to hold) (Gossip Sisters)
Small bells (2) (to ring when the door "opens") (Narrator)
Ring with ring box (Narrator as General Store Owner)
Mixing bowl & spoon (Thought-girl)
Bunches of wildflowers (3) (Neckties)
Flour sack (to hold flowers) (Neckties)
Barber's mug and brush (Narrator)
Barber's strap and razor (Narrator)
Barber's towel (to put around Neckties' neck) (Gossip Sister)
Matches (Selena)

Candle (Selena)
Paper bags (4 or more for Narrators to crinkle and make
  crackling fire sounds)

Sequence Eight:
Assorted burlap bags, bundles, saddle bags, knapsacks,
  trunks, and crates of belongings (Cast)
Satchels (2) (Neckties)
Saddle bag (Thought-girl)
Washboard (Sadie)
Bag of belongings (Sadie)
Hat (Sadie)
Basket of belongings with the diary tucked inside (The
  Mama)
Carpet bag (The Mama)
Knapsack (The Mama)
Bag of belongings (Sadie)
Small, white lily (Narrator)

SOUND CUES

Cue	Effect
A	Crashes/rumbles of thunder
B	Ship's siren
C	Thunder (continuous distant rumbles)
D	Single thunder crack
	(2 different versions)
E	Single thunder crack
F	Noon whistle
G	Night crickets (tape loop)
H	Forest fire (optional)

Script Cues

Cue 1: NARRATOR: "Until she arrived in Oregon, in the
summer of 1904."   (page 14)

A & B

Cue 2: MAN: "Just gone! Now, git in the lifeboat while
there's still time."   (page 15)

B down

Cue 3: MRS. POTTER: "Who's out there at this hour?"
                                                  (page 17)

A

Cue 4: MAN: "Yer one tough Mrs."
MRS. POTTER: "I have ta be."   (page 17)

C up

Cue 5: MRS. POTTER: "Then … leave 'er."
NARRATOR: "And … he did." (page 17)
X down slowly

Cue 6: MRS. POTTER: "If the timber wolves don't eat cha, the bears will. (page 18)
D

Cue 7: OPAL: "But, my name is Françoise." (page 20)
E

Cue 8: After "And Conquer the Land" (page 34)
F

Cue 9: GIRL THAT HAS NO SEEING: "What for?"
OPAL: "So I can teach you to see without eyes!"(page 60)
G

Cue 10: OPAL: "Sky color." (page 63)
G down

Cue 11: NARRATOR: "A small flame is ignited."(page 90)
H up slowly

Cue 12: As the lumber camp folks beat out the fire
(page 90)
H down slowly

In the New York production the Narrators created the remaining sound effects—the wolf howling, a night bird calling, a branch snapping, the whoosh of wind, the grinder squeaking, the fire crackling, etc., and Opal created the squeak of Felix Mendelssohn.

PROGRAM NOTES

Producing groups may wish to include the following articles in their show programs

(Adapted from *Opal Whiteley: The Unsolved Mystery,* by Elizabeth Bradburne Lawrence)

Opal lived in the home of a lumberman and his wife in the woods of Oregon at the turn of the century, where she wrote her childhood diary on scraps of paper—brown paper bags, the backs of envelopes—anything she could get hold of.

After leaving University, she wrote a nature book, which she took to the *Atlantic Monthly* hoping it might be published. The editor was intrigued by Opal's vivid childhood recollections and asked if she had kept a diary.

The diary had been torn up, but Opal had kept the pieces. She painstakingly put them together and it was published in 1920, in America, and in England. Then it was forgotten, until introduced once more by a B.B.C. broadcast forty years later.

In the meantime, Opal's attention had been drawn to a number of French words and phrases in her diary. Eventually she came to feel that her real father had been Prince Henry of Orleans (Henri D'Orleans), the one-time heir to what would have been the throne of France.

Since then, she has been known in England as Princesse Françoise Marie de Bourbon Orleans. She died in February 1992, in a hospital near London, where she lived well into her nineties, still certain that her father was Henri D'Orleans and that her name was Françoise.

The importance of Opal and her diary is not the mystery of who she was, fascinating as this is, but in the insight her diary gives into the inner life of childhood.

— Elizabeth Bradburne Lawrence

AUTHOR'S OPAL PROGRAM NOTES

I had the privilege of knowing Françoise D'Orleans—
visiting her in England on many occasions for over a
decade.

During these meetings, she told me about her diary and
her life. And I told her about my musical—which she
referred to as my "opera." She seemed to enjoy the songs
I played for her and was eager to answer questions that
would help shape my work. Our conversations lasted for
hours—I, taking frantic notes, while she, though old in
body, effused with the wide-eyed enthusiasm of a girl.

As the years went by, I eventually ran out of
questions, and my continuing visits grew out of
friendship rather than scholarship.

Françoise died during the second week of rehearsals
for the New York production of OPAL.

OPAL is dedicated to a friend who made earth glad.

PRODUCTION NOTES

OPAL is presented by a group of narrators, who tell the story through mime, imagination, sound effects, simple props, and by transforming themselves into various characters.

The production should be simple, spare, and magically theatrical—like *Our Town* or *Nicholas Nickleby* with elements of *Story Theatre*.

The scenery should be symbolic rather than literal. Although it's possible to perform OPAL on a bare stage, here are some suggestions:

There might be an all-purpose playing area laid with rough-hewn planks. It might be raked or elevated, as Opal will often be crouched on the ground relating to her pig.

There should be no attempt at realistic trees—painted or sculpted. Instead, the forest should be represented by very tall, rough poles.

The poles might be at the sides and rear of the central playing area; be randomly staggered and tilted; and be spaced so the actors can wander among them, and, perhaps, on occasion climb them. There should be several short,wide poles representing tree stumps that actors can sit on.

In the Lamb's production, the designer enhanced the deep forest effect by painting the cyclorama and side flats with subtle, pale silhouettes of tree trunks, done in a primitive style.

There should be no full room settings; no doors, walls, windows, or beds. Instead, a simple chair or a few props placed on stage by the actors themselves should be used to indicate place. The scenes should change cinematically—one scene dissolving to the next without pause.

The set should be earthy and rugged.

The lighting should be very evocative, colorful, and expressive—the dreamlike prologue; the storm at sea; the expansive brilliance of the out-of-doors; the bright comedy of the schoolhouse and the baby scene; the mystery of the deep forest; the bleakness of winter; the warmth of summer; the nightmarish horror of the meat-grinder; the smoke and flames of the forest fire; the eerie, burned forest; and the mystical discovery of the lily among the ashes.

The lighting should be used to open up the stage for outdoor scenes and to close down and define the space of indoor scenes.

The costumes evoke the ruggedness and poverty of lumber camp life and the opulence and elegance of Opal's former life in the "faraway lands."

The narrators' basic costume is lumber camp garb, to which they make small, fast additions or changes as they become various characters. They may add a hat, a poncho, a cape, a coat or scarf. The Gossip Sisters don half glasses and perhaps Victorian capes; The General Store Owner dons a visor and shop apron; the School Children don such things as a girl's hair ribbon, pig-tails, boys' bowties and collars, etc.

The sets, costumes, and lighting should suggest a year of season changes, from summer to summer.

The props should be things of work and reality: saws, axes, brooms, lanterns, crates, barrels, benches, blankets, rags, lanterns, branches, stools, a washtub and scrubbing board, laundry on a clothesline, wildflowers, a lily, etc. In the prologue: an elegant music box.

The animals should not be visibly represented. Instead, Opal should use mime when she pets the pig, while a male narrator creates the pig's noises. At times, a pool of light may be used to establish the pig's location. And sometimes we "see" him by the havoc he wreaks.

Opal should also mime the mouse, while she or a female narrator provide its squeak.

Many of the sound effects should be done live by the narrators, as indicated in the script—the crackling fire, the breaking of a branch, the bell on the General Store door, etc. Other sounds are best recorded—the ship's siren, the rain and thunder, crickets in the forest, etc.

The song tempos must be brisk and vigorous throughout. It is preferable that the tempos err in being too fast than too slow.

The musical underscoring that underlies most of the action of the show is integral to the work and utterly essential. It serves a descriptive, cinematic function and takes the place of scenery. The actors should early on become accustomed to the music of their scenes and approach the piece as a sort of tone poem.

General Thoughts on Staging

OPAL may be staged in a traditional, proscenium space; may utilize any area of the playing area or theatre (the aisles, balcony, etc.); and may also be staged in the round or in any non-traditional space.

The show must be fluid—with cinematic lapse dissolves and fade outs. The action must never stop or wait for a scene change.

A "sequence," as used in the script, refers to a series of scenes that take place in a continuous period of time.

A video tape of the Lamb's Theatre production is available for viewing in New York at the Performing Arts Library at Lincoln Center. It is possible to arrange a rental of their costumes and sound effects tape through the original designers.

Some Specific Ideas on Staging

THE PROLOGUE IN THE FAR-AWAY LANDS should seem distant and dreamlike. It might take place behind a scrim.

THE SHIPWRECK might be suggested by a shadowplay cast against a scrim. An upstage search-light might sweep from side to side, creating nightmarish silhouettes of the actors fighting for survival. No literal ships or lifeboats.

MRS. POTTER'S SHANTY needs almost nothing to establish it. No bed, no doorway, just an area of light and, perhaps, a chair or crate as needed.

In THE SCHOOLHOUSE SCENE, the children are played by the narrators in school children garb, sitting on crates or a bench. The teacher, as seen through Opal's eyes, is a giant. In the Lamb's production, she stood atop a barrel and wore a long skirt that reached the floor. In another production, the teacher was a very long, towering shadow projection and in another she was a towering effigy made of found objects.

SADIE McKIBBENS' SHANTY might be strung with laundry on clotheslines. A simple stool, washtub and scrubbing board establish the locale.

MICHAEL ANGELO THE FIR TREE should be represented by one or more narrators, perhaps with one or two branches, standing on graduated barrels. Opal should climb up into a male narrator's arms. If he is back-lit, it helps create a feeling of height. In the Lamb's production, the male narrators stood one behind the other on graduated barrels. One of them held a branch. The women sat on the ground, leaning against the men—their full skirts and legs forming roots. One of them snapped some kindling when Opal "broke off" the branch for the blind girl.

THE CANDLE Selena lights might be real, but some productions have used a battery-powered light, which it more reliable and easier to "light."

When the FOREST FIRE begins the narrators surround the blind girl, representing the flames closing in on her. In some productions, the narrators have wrapped her in a large, red silk sheet that flutters as she whirls away off-stage. In one production the narrators created the fire sound by crinkling paper; in the Lamb's production, they used paper bags. The lighting creates the sensation of fire and some productions have also used smoke.

The cast creates the feeling of tall pine trees falling by slowly toppling several of the poles and laying them on the ground in random positions. In the Lamb's production, the poles that represented the fir trees were black on their upstage sides, blending into a natural wood color in front. During the forest fire scene, the cast members rotated the poles, revealing the blackened side to the audience.

The fire has the effect of "wrecking" and stripping the set. It should remain that way for the remainder of the play, while changes in lighting define subsequent shifts of locale and mood.

NOTES ON THE SCENIC DESIGN

In designing the Lamb's Theatre production, we created a neutral acting space that could function as interior or exterior with minimal changes of furniture (crates, barrels, etc.) or dressing (laundry lines, lanterns, etc.) to ensure a smooth flow of scene transitions. It was racked and somewhat elevated, as Opal is often down on the floor with her pig.

We surrounded this space with a painted, stylized pine forest on the cyclorama and side flats, which, through lighting changes, could create a range of atmospheres—from warmly encircling to threatening. This also served to reflect Opal's own emotional states. The forest interpenetrated the acting area with free-standing tree trunks, which were rotated to reveal a charred side after the forest fire.

The approach was one of suggestive simplicity, with actors and props establishing transitions in a theatrical, seamless way.

FAVORITE MUSICALS *from*

"The House of Plays"

A FINE AND PRIVATE PLACE

(All Groups) Book & Lyrics by Erik Haagensen. Music by Richard Isen. Adapted from the novel by Peter S. Beagle. 3m., 2f, (may be played by 2m., 2f.) + 1 raven (may be either m. or f.) Ext. setting. "The grave's a fine and private place,/But none, I think, do there embrace." Little did you know, Andrew Marvell, that someday, someone would come up with a charming love story, set in a graveyard, about two lost souls who are buried there, who meet and fall in love. Also inhabiting the cemetery is an eccentric old man who has the gift of being able to see and converse with the inhabitants of the graves, as well as with a raven who swoops in at mealtimes with some dinner he has swiped for the old guy. Also present from time to time is a delightful old Jewish widow, whose husband Morris is buried in the cemetery. She often stops by to tell Morris what's new. Her name is Gertrude, and it is soon apparent that she also stops by to flirt with old Jonathan Rebeck (she doesn't know he actually *lives* there). A crisis arises when it appears the young couple will be separated. The young man, it seems, has been deemed a suicide and, as such, he must be removed from consecrated ground. Their only hope is Jonathan; but to help them Jonathan must come out in the open. Had we but world enough, and time, we would tell you how Jonathan manages to salvage the romance; but we'll just have to hope the above story intrigues you enough to examine the delightful libretto and wonderfully tuneful music for yourself. A sell-out, smash hit at the Goodspeed in Connecticut and, later, at the American Stage Co. in New Jersey (the professional theatre which premiered *Other People's Money),* this happy, whimsical, sentimental, up-beat new show will delight audiences of all ages. . **(#8154)**

NEW FROM SAMUEL FRENCH, INC.

SMOKE ON THE MOUNTAIN
Musical
All Groups

Book by Constance Ray. Conceived by Alan Bailey. Music & lyrics by various authors. 4m., 3f. Int. setting. Imagine a combination of *Pump Boys and Dinettes* and *Talking With* if you want to know about this daffy, delightful new show. We are at the Mt. Pleasant (North Carolina) Baptist Church in 1938, at a Saturday Night Gospel Sing arranged by Pastor Mervin Oglethorpe, a young and enthusiastic minister who also works part time in the local pickle factory, who very cautiously wants to bring his congregation into the "modern world" by (gasp!) having a concert in church! Clearly, many of the, shall we say, "less-square" members of the congregation (us in the audience) think this is a swell idea; but not Miss Maude and Miss Myrtle, two elderly spinsters who are the church's chief benefactors, who are in attendance to make sure nobody enjoys themselves. The evening's entertainment is provided by the Sanders Family Gospel Singers, who perform a slew of standard bluegrass gospel songs, from "Church in the Wildwood" to "I'm Using My Bible As a Roadmap." Between songs, the family members "witness" by telling personal stories—some quirkily humorous and others downright moving—that relate to their trials of faith. A huge success at the McCarter Theatre in Princeton (where it won over even our cynical Editor), *Smoke on the Mountain* was subsequently successfully produced in New York by the Lambs Theatre. "Wildly funny . . . so well-written is this [show] that, instead of laughing at it, I found myself laughing with it, rooting for the family, and singing along and clapping with the rest of the audience. *Smoke on the Mountain* reaches out and grabs you."—The Trentonian. "Exhilarating! A rollicking blend of monologues and musical numbers that adds up to a compone *Chorus Line*."—Variety. "A sophisticated audience went simply wild over *Smoke on the Mountain*."—Philadelphia Daily News. "A charming and funny celebration of Americana. With its mixture of softened cracker-barrel humor, Christian sweetness and light, and its attitude of gentle amusement at the squareness of it all, *Smoke on the Mountain* creates the same mood, at once sentimental and whimsical, [as] *Pump Boys and Dinettes*."—N.Y. Times. (#21236)